"Making difficult decisions is what management is all about. And the most important choices are rarely easy. *Managing in the Gray* provides a framework for anyone responsible for making tough decisions."

—**STEVE BURKE**, CEO, NBCUniversal

"This wonderful book is a graduate course in the science of thinking. It is rigorous and enjoyable."

—**CLAYTON CHRISTENSEN**, Professor, Harvard Business School; author, *The Innovator's Dilemma* and *How Will You Measure Your Life?*

"Joseph Badaracco has got it right—leadership has to come from the heart. With insight and candor, he conveys the importance of working through managerial issues with facts and analysis, but resolving them with respect and humanity. Anyone will learn from the critical questions and useful tools of deliberation and judgment revealed in *Managing in the Gray.*"

—**JAMIE DIMON**, Chairman and CEO, JPMorgan Chase & Co.

"Every leader faces decisions that are not black or white. Badaracco draws on examples—ranging from modern-day dilemmas to the insights of ancient philosophers—to provide a useful and profound guide to dealing with problems that fall into gray areas. His book is interesting, practical, and compelling."

—**GAIL McGOVERN**, President and CEO, American Red Cross

"Leaders are most significantly defined and judged by their decisions and actions related to the toughest problems.

Managing in the Gray provides a practical, nuanced, and comprehensive framework to grapple with the toughest questions of life and business."

—**KEVIN SHARER,** former Chairman and CEO, Amgen; Senior Lecturer, Harvard Business School

"*Managing in the Gray* paves a lively and approachable path through the maze of managerial dilemmas. Using a voice that is both friendly and smart, Badaracco advises managers on not just how to think about their most vexing problems, but also how to fix them."

—**DEBORA SPAR,** President, Barnard College

"When facing difficult issues, I revisit the spirit of our founder, Konosuke Matsushita. He highlighted the importance of the 'untrapped mindset,' a precept that has a lot in common with what Joseph Badaracco writes about here. All business leaders, whatever their managerial problems, will find much to stimulate their thinking in this book."

—**KAZUHIRO TSUGA,** President, Panasonic

"*Managing in the Gray* helps managers determine what is 'good' when the 'good' is far from apparent. This is a book not just to read but to live."

—**CLARK WARNER,** former Program Director, Netezza Product Management, IBM

managing in the
GRAY

managing in the
GRAY

5 TIMELESS QUESTIONS
FOR RESOLVING YOUR
HARDEST PROBLEMS
AT WORK

Joseph L. Badaracco

HARVARD BUSINESS
REVIEW PRESS
Boston, Massachusetts

HBR Press Quantity Sales Discounts

Harvard Business Review Press titles are available at significant quantity discounts when purchased in bulk for client gifts, sales promotions, and premiums. Special editions, including books with corporate logos, customized covers, and letters from the company or CEO printed in the front matter, as well as excerpts of existing books, can also be created in large quantities for special needs.

For details and discount information for both print and
ebook formats, contact booksales@harvardbusiness.org,
tel. 800-988-0886, or www.hbr.org/bulksales.

The web addresses referenced in this book were live and correct at the time of the book's publication but may be subject to change.

Library of Congress Cataloging-in-Publication Data

Names: Badaracco, Joseph, author.
Title: Managing in the gray : five timeless questions for resolving your hardest
   problems at work / Joseph L. Badaracco.
Description: Boston, Massachusetts : Harvard Business Review Press, [2016]
Identifiers: LCCN 2016026121 | ISBN 9781633691742 (hardcover)
Subjects: LCSH: Management—Philosophy. | Problem solving.
Classification: LCC HD31.2 .B33 2016 | DDC 658.4/03—dc23
LC record available at https://lccn.loc.gov/2016026121

ISBN: 978-1-63369-174-2
eISBN: 978-1-63369-175-9

The paper used in this publication meets the requirements of the American National Standard for Permanence of Paper for Publications and Documents in Libraries and Archives Z39.48-1992.

For my colleagues, past and present, in the
Leadership and Corporate Accountability course
at Harvard Business School, from whom
I've learned so much.

CONTENTS

1

Tools for Judgment

Gray areas are the hardest problems managers face at work. The reason, fundamentally, is that these are the hardest problems we face in life. When you have to deal with a highly uncertain, high-stakes problem, you face a challenge, not just to your skills, but to your humanity.

This book offers a powerful, practical way to resolve gray area problems. It is based on guidance that is unusual, even radical. The guidance doesn't come from successful or famous CEOs. It isn't found in the conventional wisdom that says serve the interests of the shareholders or all the stakeholders. Nor does it appear in the ever-lengthening mission statements of today's organizations. The soundest guidance, I believe, for grappling with hard, complex, uncertain practical problems is a set of five questions that men and women have turned to, across many centuries and cultures, when they faced this kind of problem. Gray areas demand your best judgment, and the five questions are, in essence, extraordinarily valuable tools for judgment.

This book explains why these questions are so useful for resolving gray area issues. It also gives extensive practical guidance for answering the questions and illustrates this guidance with a wide range of case studies of gray area problems. However, before we turn to the five questions, it is important to understand what gray area problems are and what makes them so important and so challenging.

The Challenge of Gray Areas

The more responsibility you take on at work and in life, the more often you face gray area problems, and these problems come in all shapes and sizes. For example, some are large, complex, and infrequent. Later in this book, we will look in detail at a situation faced by the CEO of a small biotech company who had learned that a new, much-needed drug might be implicated in a very rare, but deadly brain disease. He had to decide what to do—even though he lacked critical facts or even a clear definition of the problem.

In contrast, other gray area problems are small-scale, but this doesn't make them easy or unimportant. In a later chapter, we will look at a situation that confronted a senior manager in a medium-sized company. She shared an executive assistant with three managers. The assistant had worked at the company for more than thirty years and had a strong record, but her work had been slipping badly for several months. No one knew why. The other managers who relied on her wanted to let her go, but the senior manager was seriously concerned that the standard HR approach—giving the assistant two weeks' notice and a small severance package—might do her irreversible harm. But these concerns told the senior manager nothing about what she should do about the assistant, the work that wasn't getting done, or her disagreement with the other managers.

What all gray areas have in common, whether they are major or minor, is how we experience them. When you face a gray area problem, you have usually done a lot of hard work—on your own and often with other people—to understand a problem or a situation. You've assembled all the data, information, and expert advice you can reasonably get. You've analyzed everything carefully. But critical facts are still missing, and people you know and trust disagree about what to do. And, in your own mind, you keep going back and forth about what is really going on and about the right next steps.

These situations can be dangerous traps—organizational versions of the primeval tar pits that swallowed up the fearsome saber-toothed tigers. You can easily get bogged down in a gray area as you try to figure out what is going on. Even worse, you can get lost or be paralyzed by complexities and uncertainties. On the other hand, if you act too quickly, you can make a mistake with serious consequences: other people get hurt, performance suffers, and your career stalls.

Gray areas are particularly risky today because of the seductive power of analytical techniques. Many of the hard problems now facing managers and companies require sophisticated techniques for analyzing vast amounts of information. It is tempting to think that, if you can just get the right information and use the right analytics, you can make the right decision. It can also be tempting to hide out from tough decisions or disguise the exercise of power by telling other people that the numbers tell the whole story and that there is no choice about what to think or do. But serious problems are usually gray. By themselves, tools and techniques won't give you answers. You have to use your judgment and make hard choices.

These choices often come with serious emotional and psychological risks. When you face really hard decisions, there is no way to escape the personal responsibility of choosing, committing, acting, and living with the consequences. An MBA student presciently described this challenge by saying, "I don't want to be a businessman claiming to be a decent human being. I want to be a decent human being claiming to be a businessman."

On the other hand, when you meet these challenges and resolve a gray area problem successfully, you are making truly important contributions to your organization, other people, your career, and your sense of yourself. Hard, messy, high-stakes problems get delegated upward in organizations and land on managers' desks. Go back for a moment to the situation involving the older employee. Ask yourself what you would do. Your assistant's work has been slipping for months. You don't know why, and perhaps she doesn't either. Laws, regulations, and company policies set parameters on what you can do, but you still face some very tough questions.

Will you find another job for her, somewhere in the organization, or will you lay her off? How much and what type of severance and support will she get? Can you treat her with respect and compassion, when you are taking away her livelihood? These are all hard management questions, and you have to answer them one way or another. And behind these decisions is a profound social decision that society has delegated to you: given this employee's age and failing performance, you may be deciding that her work life has come to an end. In short, when you do a good job of resolving a gray area issue like this one, you are doing the heavy lifting—not just for your organization, but for other people and the society in which you live.

At the same time, when you grapple successfully with a gray area problem, you are testing and developing your skills as a manager. A basic test of whether you are ready for more responsibility in an organization isn't how well you manage routine situations; it is how well you handle really hard, uncertain, important challenges. This is because gray area problems are the core of a manager's work. As you meet these challenges, you build your experience and confidence, and you add lines to the informal, unwritten résumé that circulates inside organizations and determines who gets promotions. Good bosses recognize and reward people who handle the tough, gray area problems well. And, when you meet these challenges, you are also becoming a good boss yourself—by serving as a role model for the people who work for you.

Gray areas are basically organizational versions of the classic Gordian knot: that is, they are dense tangles of important, complicated, and uncertain considerations. As such, they can be some of the hardest work you have to do as a manager, and they can feel like a serious burden. At the same time, like the

Gordian knot, they can be compelling challenges that show you and others what you are capable of doing. According to myth, Alexander the Great became so frustrated with the Gordian knot that he unsheathed his sword and sliced through it but, as a manager, you don't have this option. So what is the best way to deal with the gray area problems you face?

The Five Questions

The answer, in its shortest form, can be stated in a single sentence: *when you face a gray area problem at work, you should work through it as a manager and resolve it as a human being.*

Working through gray area problems as a manager doesn't mean acting like the boss or a bureaucrat. And it doesn't mean having a particular job on an organization chart. Management is basically an extraordinarily effective way of getting things done, inside and outside organizations. At its core, managing simply means working with and through other people to accomplish something. Approaching a gray area as a manager typically means working with other people to get the right information on a problem, analyze the data thoughtfully and rigorously, and look for practical solutions to problems.

But, with gray areas, this first step isn't enough. Information, analysis, and discussion don't resolve the problem. You still don't know what to do. When this happens, you have to take a second step: you have to resolve the problem as a human being. This means grappling with the problem, not just as an analyst or a manager or a leader, but as a person. It means making decisions on the basis of your judgment—which means drawing on your intelligence, feelings, imagination, life experience, and, at a deeper level, your sense of what really matters at work and in life.

This second step may sound simple, but it isn't. We often hear that, when we face tough decisions, we should follow our moral compass, emulate a role model, follow the guidance in our organization's mission statement, or do what passes the "newspaper test" and ask if we would be comfortable seeing our actions reported in the paper, or just do the right thing. But there are no quick solutions to gray area problems. If there were, we would have them on laminated cards in our wallets.

Algorithms can't solve the hard human problems of life and work. Managers who face these problems have to learn all they can from information, data, experience, and rigorous analysis. Then they also have to think deeply—as human beings—about what they really should do. Resolving gray area problems as a human being means asking yourself the right questions and working hard to develop your own answers. These questions are the indispensable tools for deliberation and judgment. There are five of them, and this book explains them in depth.

Why do these questions help and what makes them so important? In essence, they are the questions that thoughtful men and women have relied on, for many centuries and across many cultures, when they had to grapple with hard, complex, uncertain practical problems. The questions reflect profound insights about human nature, our common life together, and what counts as a good life. Understood fully and used together, the questions are valuable tools for guiding your judgment when you have to make a decision about a gray area problem.

You may be wondering if there really could be just a few questions that actually cut to the core of really hard problems. Why would this be the case? There is no definitive answer but, as you will see in the following chapters, there is a plausible, if controversial explanation. It says two things. One is that we human beings have a common human nature, because of Darwinian evolution or divine creation. The other is that all human communities have confronted the same basic questions about responsibility, power, shared values, and decision making—and converged on the same basic approaches.

There is no single, right way to phrase the five questions. I have spent much of the last twenty years trying to develop useful, practical tools that managers can use when they confront hard issues of leadership and responsibility. The version of the five questions in this book has been refined and tested through countless executive and MBA classes, research interviews, and counseling sessions with individual managers, as well as through research and reading. In the spirit of the great American pragmatist philosopher, William James, I have tried to develop useful, everyday tools rather than universal truths, and a practical bias runs throughout this book.

The five questions are:

What are the net, net consequences?

What are my core obligations?

What will work in the world as it is?

Who are we?

What can I live with?

It is natural to wonder why these five questions would be remarkably useful. The answer is that they have passed a demanding test. It asks if there are ways of thinking about hard decisions that have, over the centuries, engaged many of the most penetrating minds and compassionate hearts when they were searching for the right way to resolve really difficult problems. As you will see, the five questions, expressed in various ways, have engaged philosophers, ranging from Aristotle to Nietzsche; religious leaders, like Confucius and Christ; and political thinkers, like Machiavelli and Jefferson; as well as poets and even artists.

To be clear, this test does not ask whether there is some grand consensus that the great thinkers of history all accept. That would be a preposterous claim. The key question is whether there are some approaches that have consistently *engaged* many of these powerful, incisive, compassionate minds, when they tried to understand what made for good decisions and good lives. If some ways of thinking have passed this test of history and culture, then they are well worth our time and thoughtful attention.

The five questions are, in effect, important voices in a long conversation about how the world really works, what makes us truly human, and the soundest way to make difficult, important decisions. No single voice in the long conversation gives us a universal truth, but each gives us valuable insights for making uncertain, high-stakes decisions. That is why these questions are such powerful tools for testing, broadening, and sharpening your judgment when you face gray area issues.

What kinds of tools are they? Philosophers, lawyers, theologians, and political theorists can sharpen each of the questions to a fine edge and wield these intellectual scalpels with brilliance. But managers need something different: they need sound, sturdy, everyday tools—like the ones in toolboxes and kitchen drawers. This comparison to tools may seem like a passing metaphor, but it actually reflects a long intellectual tradition at Harvard Business School, which has aimed, for more than a century, to develop important, useful ideas for managers. Professor Fritz Henderson, one of the school's intellectual pioneers, believed that most useful theory for managers was "not a philosophical theory, nor a grand effort of the imagination, nor a quasi-religious dogma, but a modest pedestrian affair or perhaps I had better say, a useful walking stick to help on the way."[1]

The rest of the book will show the down-to-earth practicality of the five questions. Each chapter focuses on one and begins by explaining why it is so important for really understanding the full human dimensions of gray area problems. The rest of each chapter then explains practical guidelines—also rooted in long-standing, widely shared views of our common humanity—for using each question when you face a gray area issue.

A Working Philosophy

Used alone, the five questions are valuable tools for judgment, but taken together, they are much more. They give us an important philosophy of management—a way of understanding what managers really do and why it matters. This philosophy doesn't consist of abstract concepts, binding principles, or an all-purpose template. It is a working philosophy. It is a disposition, an attitude, a habit of mind, and a guide to action.

This philosophy says that the core of management work is resolving hard problems in practical ways. It also says that, if you want to be a successful manager today, you have to be able to grapple with complexities of all kinds, draw sound conclusions from a wide range of information, and use sophisticated analytical tools. But, because gray area challenges are the core of management work, these analytical skills aren't enough. You also need a humanist perspective on your work.

The word "humanist" can sound like something from a traditional college catalog, but the thinking behind it is directly relevant to making hard decisions at work and in life. Humanism has a long tradition. Its roots go back to ancient writers, and it became a strong force, intellectually and politically, during the Renaissance.* Humanists asked basic questions and tried to get down to the fundamentals about what truly matters in life, what motivates people, and how the world really works. These fundamentals become central when you have worked through a gray area problem as a manager and now must resolve it as a human being.

This humanist philosophy of management doesn't try to force the complex, messy challenge of resolving hard problems into some final, definitive analytical framework. It says you have to examine a problem from a range of perspectives. You have to rely on your judgment, which reflects your

---

*Appendix A gives a historical and philosophical overview of humanism as it is used in this book.

thinking, feelings, intuitions, experiences, hopes, and fears. And it says that, in the end, the right answer to a gray area problem is what you decide is right—but only after working through a problem in its full analytical and human dimensions. This way of thinking is hard to distill into a few words or phrases but it is, I believe, the tacit worldview of the successful, responsible men and women who find ways to navigate the gray areas all around us.

2

What Are the Net, Net Consequences?

When the US Marine Corps trains young officers, it tells them "the radio is your weapon." In other words, they won't be fighting on their own, with rifles, handguns, and bayonets. The radio is their weapon because, as officers, they will fight by leading other soldiers.[1] The same is true for you as a manager. Your organization—whether it is a team, a department, or an entire organization—amplifies the impact of the decisions you make. This is why the first question asks you to think hard about the net, net consequences of what you might do, when you face a gray area problem. This may sound like common sense. Of course, you should think about the consequences of your decisions. Everyone should. But this reaction can be profoundly deceptive, even for experienced, successful managers. To see this, consider a remarkable series of events that began in 1996. Late that year, something extraordinary happened: an American business executive came to be viewed as a national hero.

The executive was named Aaron Feuerstein. His company, which made and sold textiles, was called Malden Mills, and its best-known product was Polartec fabric. In December 1996, while Feuerstein and his family were celebrating his seventieth birthday, he got an urgent phone call. The main plant at Malden Mills was on fire. Feuerstein got into his car and drove north from Boston toward his company. He first saw the flames when he was several miles from the plant. When Feuerstein arrived, the facility was an inferno that reminded him of the firebombing of Dresden in World War II.[2]

Because of the fire, Feuerstein faced a profound gray area decision. He didn't know how much he would collect in insurance compensation. He didn't know how much business he would lose to competitors while he was rebuilding. He didn't know if Malden Mills would even survive, if he rebuilt a textile plant in New England, because much of the industry had already moved to low-wage countries in Asia. Feuerstein didn't even know if he was the right person to lead the company into its next phase.

Despite all these uncertainties, Feuerstein almost immediately made a personal commitment to rebuild the entire facility. The new plant would utilize state-of-the-art technology and employ the same workforce. The cost would ultimately be more than $400 million. Insurance covered $300 million, and the rest was bank loans. Feuerstein also announced he would continue paying his workers' salaries during the rebuilding, even if they had no work to do. These were the decisions that catapulted Feuerstein to national prominence.

At a time when many US jobs were being outsourced, Feuerstein had made a strong commitment to American workers and the struggling communities in which many of them lived. He received widespread media attention, a dozen honorary degrees, and was a guest at President Clinton's State of the Union address in 1997. Then, just a few years later, Malden Mills filed for bankruptcy. New owners and managers took over the business, but it never recovered.

There is a sad, almost tragic, irony here. If you met Aaron Feuerstein, you would probably view him as most people did: as a generous, warm, honest individual. Despite his wealth and age, he lived modestly and worked hard. When a journalist asked Feuerstein if he wanted to have more money, he replied, "What am I going to do, eat more?"[3] After the fire, Feuerstein genuinely wanted to do what was best for his workers, their communities, and the company. In other words, he thought the decision to rebuild would have all the right consequences. Instead, it bankrupted Malden Mills. Feuerstein's character, dedication, and altruism led nowhere. And the reason, it now seems, is that he failed to make use of the first great humanist question.

This question asks you to think broadly and deeply about the full, all-in consequences of your options. So what was this question asking Aaron Feuerstein to think about? What makes it such an important question? And how can you use this question as a tool for judgment when you face a gray area problem?

Thinking Broadly and Thinking Deeply

To understand why the first question matters and what it is really asking, we will turn briefly to two important philosophers and social reformers and, in particular, to the shattering life experience that shaped the ideas of one of them. The first philosopher is Jeremy Bentham, who lived in England from 1748 to 1832. Even if you don't recognize his name, you are probably familiar with his central idea. Bentham believed that the right way to work through really hard, important problems was to look as broadly as possible and ask what would promote "the greatest happiness for the greatest number of people." In other words, before you make an important decision, look at its consequences—in terms of happiness—for everyone you will affect.

But what is happiness? For Bentham, the answer was simple: happiness is pleasure. In other words, to be a responsible person and make good decisions, all you have to do is think thoroughly and objectively about what will produce the greatest pleasure and the least pain. There is no formula for this, so you have to make judgments. But your basic objective is clear. You have to think broadly. This means looking at legal and economic consequences and also looking beyond them. It means looking at consequences for the people in your organization and looking beyond them as well. What matters are all the consequences for everyone affected by your decision—and this means *everyone*.

Today, we are all disciples of Jeremy Bentham. We often think about problems—everyday problems and huge questions of government policy—in terms of cost and benefits or costs and risks. This means looking at all the options, assessing their likely consequences, and trying to find the option that is best for everyone. This approach is an altogether useful and responsible way of making decisions, but Bentham's thinking has a profound flaw. It encourages us to think broadly, but not deeply.

John Stuart Mill, perhaps the most important philosopher in the English-speaking world in the 1800s, discovered the severity of this flaw, not by sitting in a chair and thinking, but by having his life painfully derailed. Mill was the brilliant son of a domineering, highly intellectual father, who imposed a rigorous educational program on him. The young Mill was kept away from other children, began learning Greek at the age of three, Latin at eight, and Aristotle's logic at twelve. Mill's radical training continued until he was twenty, and then he suffered a massive emotional breakdown. Today, Mill's collapse would probably be diagnosed as acute depression. And anyone who has suffered from depression will understand why Mill chose these lines, from a poem called "Dejection," to describe his misery:

> *A grief without a pang, void, dark and drear,*
> *A drowsy, stifled, unimpassioned grief,*
> *Which finds no natural outlet or relief*
> *In word, or sigh, or tear.*[4]

Later in life, Mill blamed his breakdown on his intense, narrow, highly intellectualized upbringing.

Mill's reaction to this experience was extraordinary. His grueling education and devastating collapse would have crushed many people, but Mill soldiered on and recast his life. He rejected his father's plan for him to attend Oxford or Cambridge. He dramatically widened his reading and thinking, became devoted to Romantic poetry, and ultimately worked for several decades in a "day job" as a clerk in the British East India Company. Mill also wrote books and articles on a wide range of topics and became Britain's most important nineteenth-century philosopher and public intellectual.

Why does Mill's journey in life matter to us? Essentially, it's that he accepted Bentham's mandate to think broadly about hard decisions but rejected Bentham's focus on happiness. Mill's painful experience taught him that we have to think broadly *and deeply*, if we want to make good decisions and live good lives. Mill agreed with Bentham that, to make a good decision, you should think about everybody affected. You should be as objective as possible and put aside your own self-interest. And you should think carefully and analytically and be as specific as you can about the consequences of your choices.

But Mill added a crucial humanist insight: be careful not to oversimplify, and don't be a reductionist. Life is a rich canvas, not a cartoon, and there is far more to human experience than pleasure and pain. Thinking about the full consequences of the decision means thinking deeply—trying to understand consequences in terms of everything that matters to us as human beings: hope, joy, security, freedom from hazards, health, friendship and love, risk, suffering, and dreams.

Thinking deeply isn't easy. It takes time and imagination, empathy and compassion. But it is profoundly realistic and important. For Mill, it was actually the best way to live, as well as the right way to make decisions. In Mill's words, it is better "to be a human being dissatisfied than a pig satisfied; better to be Socrates dissatisfied than a fool satisfied."[5]

In practical terms, Mill is saying to us: If you have to make a hard decision, don't make Bentham's mistake. Don't over-simplify. Don't just focus on what you can count or price.

You should certainly think carefully and analytically. If you are a manager, you should get the best data you can, apply the relevant techniques and frameworks, consult the appropriate experts, and work the issues hard in meetings and around the water cooler. But, when you finally have to decide what to do, make sure you are also thinking concretely, imaginatively, vividly, and empathically about the consequences of your options. And, as you think, consider everything that your fellow humans need, want, fear, and really care about. That, in essence, is what the first great humanist question asks us to do.

How much weight should we give to Mill's thinking? His ideas seem sound—at least at first glance—but Mill had a bizarre childhood and a traumatic early adulthood. He may have clung to these ideas like a life preserver, but does that mean the rest of us should follow them? The answer to this question is yes, and to see why, we have to put aside the notion that these are Mill's ideas.

Mill basically did what many of the great philosophers have done. He distilled and expressed, in clear, simple language, a set of powerful ideas—ideas that run like bright threads through the thinking, reflections, and insights of many important philosophers, religious figures, and political leaders. Put differently, the ideas and insights Mill encapsulated have, for centuries, been the inspiring and shaping forces in individual lives and across societies.

For example, in China, in roughly 400 BCE, Mozi—an important Eastern philosopher and a contemporary and rival of Confucius—wrote something that could easily be a passage from Mill. "It is the business of the benevolent man," he wrote, "to seek to promote what is beneficial to the world and to eliminate what is harmful."[6] Mozi believed in what he called "inclusive care." Good men and good rulers, he said, were concerned—in their decisions and throughout their lives—about everyone in their communities, and not just themselves, their families, and their political allies.[7]

The power of this idea, during the ensuing centuries and millennia, is hard to exaggerate. It has been rediscovered again and again and applied to a vast range of situations. It also reinforces other central ideas, like justice and fairness. For example, the idea of thinking about the consequences for everyone is a basic ideal of democratic societies. You can see it in the great speeches of many leaders and the foundational documents of most countries. They refer explicitly and repeatedly to serving the needs, interests, and aspirations of everyone in a society or a country. Today, it is the powerful rallying cry of countless groups, all around the world, as they seeking to reform their governments or throw off oppression.

The basic idea, which is Mill's idea, is that everyone counts the same. This is because all of us can suffer, face risk, and carry hard burdens, and we can all feel pleasure, delight, satisfaction, and pride. Religious believers reach the same conclusion—that everyone matters—because they see everyone as a creature of God. And this religious precept actually resonates with a basic tenet of evolutionary theory.

British philosopher and historian David Hume sketched this idea more than two centuries ago, when he observed, "There is some benevolence, however small, infused into our bosom; some spark of friendship for humankind; some particle of the dove kneaded into our frame, along with the elements of the wolf and the serpent."[8] The contemporary version of this idea says that early humans and prehumans, the creatures who survived and ultimately evolved into us, probably had cooperative instincts. These would have made it easier for them to work together to collect and store food, find shelter, care for their young, and fight off attacks. In contrast, the less cooperative prehumans were less likely to survive because they squandered precious time and energy fighting each other.

In short, the first great humanist question is a powerful and perhaps even instinctive way to think about complex, uncertain, high-stakes decisions. The question succinctly expresses the wisdom and guidance that have endured and mattered profoundly for many centuries. It says to men and women struggling with gray area problems that they should think broadly and deeply about the full human consequences of a decision. This means asking what you will be doing *for* other people and *to* other people, depending on the option you choose. Then choose the plan of action with the best net, net consequences. Thinking and acting this way makes for good decisions and a good life.

The Practical Challenges

The first question seems directly relevant to thinking through gray area problems—as long as we put aside two serious problems. One problem is out in the real world, and the other is inside our heads.

The real-world problem is that we can't see the future. None of us has a crystal ball, so how are we supposed to assess the full, all-in consequences? It's a cliché that the future is uncertain but, because we like to have some sense of control over our lives, we often underestimate how uncertain the future actually is. This challenge is so great that highly regarded experts do bad jobs of prognosticating, *even in their own fields.*[9] The reason, in many cases, is the reality of complex interactions. Much of today's world resembles a vast pinball machine. A manager makes a decision—the equivalent of firing a pinball—and then it bangs around unpredictably, setting off other chains of events, and some of these, in turn, interact with each other. As a result, it is very hard to know where the pinball will end up.

Experts aren't the only people with this problem. Robert Merton, a highly regarded sociologist, posited what came to be known as Merton's Law. This is the disconcerting proposition that the unintended, secondary consequences of decisions and actions—ranging from our minor, everyday choices to massive public policy decisions—often outweigh the consequences we intend.[10] This may, in fact, have been part of Aaron Feuerstein's problem. How was he supposed to know what might happen, years down the road, when he decided to rebuild his operations? The thinkers who focused on consequences lived in simpler eras. Perhaps Mozi would have been less confident about foreseeing beneficial consequences if he could have stepped into a time machine and glimpsed the complex, fluid, confusing, and incomprehensively interdependent world we live in today.

The second serious practical challenge is in our heads. We just aren't very good at thinking rationally and objectively—not just about the unknowable future, but about the past and even the present. Gray areas sometimes bring out strong emotions and make it hard to think soundly, but that is just the tip of the iceberg. The challenge runs much deeper.[11]

The problem is that our minds can be viewed as having two basic systems for making decisions. One is a recent evolutionary development. It is conscious, analytical, and rational. It looks objectively at facts and ways of framing or analyzing those facts. The other system has been part of human nature for much longer. It is unconscious and instinctive. It was probably crucial to the survival of our distant ancestors. When we make decisions, which system do we use? Countless careful studies indicate that our subterranean, instinctive decision system dominates the rational parts of our minds.

A truly remarkable example is a recent study involving Israeli parole judges. Researchers found that the first prisoner they reviewed in the morning had a 65 percent chance of parole. This was also true for the first prisoner reviewed after lunch. In contrast, the prisoners considered just before lunch and at the end of the day had little chance of parole. These judges were experts, they were trained in the law, they were men and women of integrity, they were following clear standards, and they knew their decisions were important. Nevertheless, some powerful, unconscious forces profoundly shaped their deliberations.[12]

What are these unconscious forces? Researchers in a wide range of fields—including cognitive neuroscience, psychology, and linguistics—are just beginning to sort them out. And the answer may be that there is *no* simple answer. Our minds, it now seems, consist of myriad, semi-independent modules, each of which evolved to handle a different task. Some help us walk upright; others sense danger; others remember, plan, and love. These modules seem to operate simultaneously and often clash with each other. As a result, our minds resemble "a noisy parliament of competing factions."[13]

The great thinkers who advocated some version of the first question seem to have assumed a stable, predictable world and stable, rational minds. Perhaps they would have rethought their ideas, or even abandoned them, if they lived today and saw the complexity and turbulence around us and inside us. These challenges to the first question are clearly serious. So can we really use it as a practical tool for judgment?

Practical Guidance: Get the Process Right

The answer to this question is yes, and the rest of this chapter presents five steps you can take to deal with the practical challenges and use the question to improve your judgment on gray area problems.

Stop the Train

This first guideline for understanding the net, net consequences in a particular situation says simply: When you have to make a gray area decision, avoid drawing conclusions and try to keep others from doing the same thing. Don't assume you or anyone else can quickly see where the pinball will end up and what the full consequences of a complex, uncertain decision will be. Try instead to put aside your initial intuitions about what the right answer is.

The Malden Mills story shows why this guidance is so important—because Aaron Feuerstein didn't follow it. After the terrible fire, he felt a heavy burden of responsibility. Thirty-three of his workers had been injured, twelve critically, and hundreds of people were about to lose incomes they really needed. Feuerstein wanted to do all he could to help his employees. He felt a deep and urgent sense of obligation to them. That is why he made the quick commitment to rebuild everything. Feuerstein's instinct was exemplary, but it was also a runaway train.

The world is, of course, a much better place when men and women with talent, power, and wealth feel a strong sense of responsibility for the livelihoods and lives of other people—and this is the core concern of the first humanist question—but these admirable personal commitments can also lead them, and us, in the wrong direction. We want to deal with a problem head-on, but we overestimate our knowledge and our judgment. When Feuerstein did this, he exposed himself, his company, and its employees to the vagaries of a perilous, uncertain future and the all-too-human frailties of his own thinking and instincts.

Several years ago, researchers asked a large sample of Americans whether several prominent individuals were likely to go to heaven. Mother Teresa was near the top of the list, with 72 percent expecting her to achieve eternal bliss. But the highest probability of going to heaven was the choice "Yourself," with 89 percent.[14] A recent study of prison inmates found that they rated themselves higher than non-prisoners on kindness, generosity, self-control, and morality.[15] Studies like these are part of the mountain of evidence for our deep instinct to overrate, sometimes wildly, our personal capabilities, judgment, and moral integrity.

In other words, we humans have a strong self-enhancement bias.[16] It may have contributed to our survival as a species, by encouraging our forebears to take on hard challenges, but its risks rise steeply as problems and the consequences of options for dealing with them grow more complex and uncertain. Hence, the first step toward grasping the net, net consequences is to forget about cracking the case or displaying your intellectual acuity. Try instead to see yourself modestly and realistically, as one of the fallible human creatures depicted throughout serious history and literature, as well as in contemporary social science. This will help you avoid mistakes and clear the way for the second step.

Focus on Process

When you face a gray area problem, your basic task is getting the process right. Gray area problems are rarely resolved in a flash of intuitive brilliance from a single individual. As one very successful and widely respected CEO put it, "The lonely leader on Olympus is really a bad model." Process is critical for gray area problems because you may never know whether you actually made the right decision. All you can know is that you worked on the problem in the right way.

What is process? It is basically what good managers spend their time doing. Management is simply working with and through other people to accomplish goals. To resolve a gray area issue, you have to carefully manage how you and others tackle the problem. This is a theme you will hear, again and again, as we look at ways to use the five questions as tools for judgment.

This approach can seem odd or dismaying. After all, organizational processes have dismal associations: process conjures up complex diagrams with arrows and feedback loops and interminable, soul-destroying meetings. But consider a striking statement made by Alexander Bickel, one of the foremost modern scholars of the US Constitution. Bickel wrote, "The highest morality is almost always the morality of process."[17] This could sound like the motto of a career bureaucrat, but it is actually a profound insight because, when you face a gray area problem, *how* you work on the problem can be as important as *what* you ultimately decide to do.

Why is this the case? The reason is all around us. We live in a world of marvelous social inventions called organizations. They are big and small, public and private, formal and informal. Organizations are our ambient life-support system. Without them, our homes would have mud floors, our work would be long and harsh, and our lives painful and short. It is managers who make organizations work, and they do this by getting the process right. Managers and process make our world go round.

We overlook this reality because we live in a world that prizes leaders and views managers as second-class citizens. Leaders, we hear so often, have visions of how things can be, they captivate others with their passion and commitment, and sometimes they change the world. In contrast, managers keep the trains running on time. The conventional wisdom says they are plumbers and mechanics. They run meetings, create agendas, and do budgets. They are "the dull step-children" of organizations.[18] One of today's reigning clichés puts the stereotype succinctly: leaders do the right thing, and managers do things in the right way.

This cliché is badly misleading. It ignores the fact that the great leaders of history were often effective managers who got the process right. We remember Mohandas Gandhi, Martin Luther King Jr., and Nelson Mandela for their galvanizing speeches, heroic self-sacrifice, and the millions of people they inspired. But serious biographies of great leaders show they understood the importance of process. In meeting after meeting, over months and years, they poured time and energy into managing the movements and organizations that amplified their impact on the world.

For example, we might have never heard King's "I Have a Dream" speech if he hadn't spent weeks beforehand forging a coalition of six fractious civil rights groups and organizing what became the March on Washington.[19] In short, if many of the great leaders had not been effective managers, we wouldn't know their names today. They succeeded because they got the process right. Doing things in the right way is usually the best way and often the only way to do the right thing.

28

The basic task, for men and women facing gray area problems, is managerial. It is working on process. This means trying to put aside initial feelings and intuitions about what the right answer is and focusing instead about how to work with and through other people to develop an answer.

Process does slow things down. But this is an advantage, not a drawback. It reduces the danger of quick decisions made in isolation. Time lets you and others think, listen, disagree, and rethink. It can let unconventional options emerge. Time lets people work together and carefully imagine second- and third-order consequences. And time lets initial, emotional reactions subside. Gray area issues demand patience, care, and diligence—and these are often critical, given the challenge of grasping the net, net consequences in gray area situations.

Get the Right People in the Room

A crucial part of getting the process right is having the right people, with the right experience and expertise, fully involved. Who are these people? The answer, of course, varies from situation to situation. Some gray area problems have to be decided quickly. If time is short and the stakes are low, the right process is a brief, candid conversation with a sensible colleague. At the other end of the spectrum, there are gray area issues like the one Aaron Feuerstein faced, with layers of complex strategic, organizational, and human issues. These problems require a wide range of judgment and experience.

Who belongs in the room, when you are dealing with a really complex gray area issue? Obviously, you want people you know and trust. You need the views of individuals who are honest, take their responsibilities seriously, and have the right background for the kind of problem you face. And, when you are trying to understand the net, net consequences in a complex situation, you need people with a "feel" for how things work in your organization and in the world.

An instinct for what may really be going on in complex situations is a practical talent. Imagine, for example, an experienced neonatal nurse, working late at night in an intensive care unit for premature infants. She looks over the monitors that track the babies' vital signs, and everything seems fine. Then she looks at one of the infants, and his skin color seems odd. Maybe it's just the light, she thinks, but she feels something is off. She decides to alert the other staff, they examine the child, find a serious problem, and manage to save the baby's life. Imagine an experienced firefighter. He enters a burning room with several other firefighters. Then he senses something, tells his men to run from the room, and they escape just before the floor collapses.[20]

The nurse and the firefighter felt there was more to their situations than met the eye, and they had developed this sense through years of experience. Neither was relying on a rule or a template. Both had knowledge and skills, but these were interlaced with practiced powers of observation and an aptitude for discerning patterns within complexity.[21] Neither was a technician, and both took a humanist approach to their situations: they relied on instincts honed by extensive, relevant, on-the-ground experience. This helped them sense serious consequences when others might have seen only complexity and uncertainty.

Such experts are actually all around us, but we usually don't realize it, because these everyday experts often don't have the standard degrees and résumés. Aaron Feuerstein had some of these experts around him. His senior management team had years of experience running the company, competing hard for customers in the dog-eat-dog global textile market and watching pennies in manufacturing. Over weeks or months, they could have helped Feuerstein analyze and grasp the all-in consequences of his options after the fire—in terms of the competition, the company's finances and economics, alternative technologies, and the company's legal obligations. Unfortunately, Feuerstein overruled these experts when they raised questions about his decision to rebuild the entire operation with state-of-the-art technology.

Pragmatic, everyday experts don't have bright lights that dispel all the gray. No one can do that. But, when you face a gray area problem, these are the people you want to pull into the process. And you find them by looking for them—ideally, before the gray area problem lands on your desk. Look around your organization and ask yourself: Who has a track record of making prudent assessments in murky situations? Who is good at framing or reframing situations in useful and revealing ways? Who is willing to work on a team, learn from others, and doesn't need to be the star? Who has the trait Jane Austen called "self-command"—so they are less likely to be carried away by their own feelings or emotional contagions spreading through a group?[22] These are the kind of people you want in the room when you grapple with gray area problems.

Work on a Simple Decision Tree

How can you structure and focus your efforts, and the efforts of everyone working with you, to understand the net, net consequences? There is, of course, no single right approach, and much depends on the specifics of situations. But, before you make a final decision, you almost always have to take an important step. You can describe the step in various ways—as looking at the big picture, isolating critical trade-offs, recognizing the rock bottom facts, or getting a view from the balcony—but these all amount to the same thing. You need to clearly see what your basic options are and the likely all-in consequences of each.

A valuable way to do this was sharply articulated more than two hundred years ago by an obscure British minister, but military commanders, merchants, and seafarers have used versions of it since antiquity. The minister was Reverend Thomas Bayes, who lived in rural England during the eighteenth century. His approach has now evolved into sophisticated decision-making theories and important areas of advanced statistics, but his core insight is a remarkably simple and useful way of distilling the net, net consequences of decisions.

Bayes directly addressed the two practical challenges to understanding these consequences: none of us has a crystal ball, and we do a poor job of thinking objectively. Bayes knew this.[23] So he suggested that we stop trying to forecast the future. Instead, he recommended that we see the future as simply a range of possibilities.

To see what Bayes meant by this, imagine what he might have said to Aaron Feuerstein: I have made my career as a minister, and I understand personal tragedy. You and your workers have suffered a catastrophic loss. I understand and admire your urgent desire to help them and their families. But you need to step back and really think through the many possible consequences of your next steps. Because so much is unknown and because you may be in the grip of powerful emotional reactions, I suggest that you try using a simple decision tree.[24] It looks like a technique, but it's really a way of thinking. It won't give you answers, but it can give you a much clearer sense of the consequences of your options.

Managers facing gray areas can create simple decision trees by taking two steps. The first is developing a list of all your options for dealing with the problem. That is, you don't start by thinking about what you *should* do, which is where Feuerstein seems to have begun. Instead, be open-minded and creative and focus on all the things you *could* do.[25] Second, work hard to flesh out the possible outcomes of each option and the odds these consequences might occur.

That description is abstract, so let's look at what it meant in the Malden Mills case. When Aaron Feuerstein decided, on the night of the fire, to rebuild everything with the latest technology, he was assuming, in effect, that he had a very peculiar decision tree. This tree had just one branch: rebuild it all. This branch, he seemed to believe, would lead to a single outcome, a successful recovery and a thriving company, and he seemed to think the odds of this outcome were very high.

Unfortunately, the branch he chose had other possible outcomes. One was a long, profitless struggle to recover. Another was the disaster that actually occurred. Any careful analysis of the textile industry in America would have indicated that both of these outcomes had significant probabilities of occurring, because so many US textile firms had met these fates. These possibilities dramatically reduced the likely value of the "rebuild everything" option. That option, properly understood, was the weighted value of three possibilities: a big success; a long, unrewarding struggle; and utter failure.

Even worse, Feuerstein didn't seem to realize his decision tree had other branches. Each was some combination of closing businesses that were failing, investing heavily in R&D for promising new products, outsourcing some production, selective rebuilding, and generous severance and retraining support for laid-off workers. Would some of these combinations have worked? No one knows. But Feuerstein and his senior managers could have worked intensely to assess these options and their odds of success—before making final decisions. This would have given them a basic decision tree. They would have seen what their options were and the possible consequences of each of them.

By doing this, they might have found branches on their decision tree that could have kept Malden Mills in business, avoided bankruptcy, and provided jobs for many workers and retraining for others. The company ultimately received about $300 million in insurance payments and $100 million from banks. These funds, spent prudently and strategically, might have enabled Feuerstein to accomplish a good deal—though not all—of what he really cared about. And, most important, if he had used some version of a decision tree to make sure he was thinking broadly and deeply, Feuerstein might have produced much better net, net consequences for everyone.

When you face a gray area problem, you don't have to create complex, precisely crafted decision trees, and you usually can't. But you can spend time and work with others to think carefully about the full range of options, outcomes, and probabilities. You can also update your assessment of the possible outcomes as you get new information. But what really matters is the mental process of looking broadly, considering the full range of possible outcomes, and thinking hard—with imagination and empathy—about each outcome and making your best judgment about the odds each outcome might occur.

Simple decision trees have many advantages, and one is encouraging you to confront ugly possibilities—something most of us are reluctant to do. One of the reasons computers beat outstanding human chess players is that they analyze every option with utterly emotionless clarity. In contrast, human beings behave like proper Victorians and avert their gaze from the consequences and scenarios that look complicated, discouraging, or harsh.[26]

In the case of Malden Mills, the ugly possibility was a prospect that an entrepreneur like Aaron Feuerstein, who had overcome grim industry trends with the brilliant introduction of Polartec, could fail badly and destroy his own company. Another ugly possibility, which Aaron Feuerstein seems to have pushed aside, was the prospect of going bankrupt, laying off his entire workforce, and devastating their community in the event his bold commitment failed.

The first great humanist question asks you to look directly at the ugly consequences. In particular, you have to look at outcomes that impose hardship and serious risk on innocent people, especially the ones who may be almost invisible to you when you are making a gray area decision. Your focus then is usually the decision itself and all its complexities and uncertainties. Often, you are under time pressure to get the problem solved. All this makes it less likely you will really look broadly and deeply. To see the risks, hazards, and damage you may be imposing on vulnerable, yet invisible people, you have to look beyond the boundaries of your organization and beyond your economic and legal obligations. This can be uncomfortable and make your decision even more complicated, but it is what Bentham, Mill, Mozi, Christ, and so many other wise and insightful minds believed was right.

Orchestrate Pushback

If you want to see the full, possible consequences of a decision, you have to do more than bring the right people together and get the analysis structured in the right way. Two factors can subvert any sound process you create. These are *groupthink* and *bossthink*. The first leads us to stifle our concerns and go along with the sentiments of a group. The second leads us to go on autopilot and agree with our bosses. To get the process right and get the consequences clear, you have to fight both of these common tendencies.

Aaron Feuerstein may have made a decisive error along these lines. A well-respected senior executive at Malden Mills strongly opposed his plan to rebuild. As a result, she was fired. Decisions like this send messages that reverberate, like strong aftershocks, throughout an organization. One message is: the boss's instincts matter more than your analysis. Another is: disagreeing with the boss, even on a complex, gray area decision, puts your job at risk. Another is: you can find safety by not diverging from whatever a group or your boss seems to be thinking.

Because groupthink and bossthink are serious problems, good managers fight them head-on. One tactic is dividing a working group into small teams and having them work separately on analysis and action plans, to encourage independent thinking. Another is asking advocates of a particular viewpoint to state the strongest reasons for disagreeing with their position. This is a way of seeing how thoroughly they have analyzed the problem.

Another tactic is appointing one or two individuals in a group to act as devil's advocate. Everyone knows what a devil's advocate is, but the familiarity of the term conceals how important this approach is for resolving hard problems. A dialectical search for truth—based on opposition and contradiction—appears in every major philosophical tradition. And the devil's advocate tactic itself is centuries old. The Catholic Church developed it during the Middle Ages to vet candidates for sainthood: a devil's advocate was formally appointed to argue against God's advocate, who supported sainthood.[27]

When you face a gray area problem, the job of the devil's advocate is to present the strongest possible arguments against views or conclusions that a group is about to agree on. For this approach to work, devil's advocates need the organizational equivalent of immunity from prosecution. This means believing that thoughtful disagreement, even with the boss, will win points rather than lose them.

The devil's advocate tactic is a highly versatile way to create pushback. For example, some military forces use "red team-blue team" exercises. These test the readiness of a group by dividing it in two and having one part attack the other—to reveal strengths and vulnerabilities.[28] President Lincoln's cabinet included several powerful political adversaries. Historian Doris Kearns Goodwin called this a "team of rivals" and concluded that it helped Lincoln make much better decisions during a crucial era in American history.[29]

Yet another valuable form of pushback is asking for "plain English." This means asking experts to explain their assessments of likely consequences in the language of ordinary mortals. This tactic can help everyone in a group grasp important elements of a situation and reduces the chances that some people will defer to abstruse analysis so they don't look dumb. The "plain English" standard can also prepare you to explain your decision, clearly and persuasively, to larger groups of non-experts, once you've made a decision and implementation begins.

All of these tactics for encouraging pushback are basically ways of helping you make sure you have really thought through the net, net consequences, when you face a gray area problem. They won't guarantee that you overcome the twin challenges of uncertainty and human fallibility—because nothing will—but they load the dice in favor of better outcomes, for you and everyone your decision will affect.

Do We Really Need More Questions?

Suppose you are facing a gray area decision and you have followed the guidance in this chapter. Aren't you now ready to make a decision? You have followed a powerful, age-old mandate—with deep roots in important religious, philosophical, and political traditions—to look broadly and deeply at the all-in consequences of your options. You've avoided rushing to judgment, worked hard on getting the right people together and setting up the right process. You've considered the full spectrum of options, odds, and outcomes, perhaps by using a rough decision tree. You've encouraged candid, critical discussion and looked hard at the ugly possibilities. What more could you do?

The first question, with its sharp focus on the consequences for everyone who will be helped and hurt by your decision, seems to be *the right way* to resolve gray area problems and an admirable way to live. Do we really need more questions and other tools for judgment? The answer to this question is unambiguously *yes*. To see why, imagine the following scenario—a playful thought experiment that dramatizes the limits and dangers of the first question.

Imagine you live in a country that takes the first question very seriously. Its leaders have carefully designed the government so its decisions follow the precepts of Mill, Mozi, Christ, and important political thinkers. What matters, above all, in this country are policies and decisions that objectively produce the best net, net consequences, and you support these policies. One evening, your doorbell rings. You open the front door and find three police officers. You invite them in, and they quickly get to the point. They tell you there are six people on life support at a nearby hospital, and all of them urgently need organ transplants. They plan to take you to the hospital, where you will become an organ donor. The government health office has done a rough decision tree and estimates that you will lose roughly forty years of life, but the others will gain hundreds of years. The officers suggest that you do the right thing and come with them voluntarily. If you don't, they will handcuff you and take you to the hospital.

What should you do? If you go along with the plan, you will die, and your loved ones and friends will grieve, though they may also be comforted, as you might be in your final moments, by the thought that your sacrifice saved six lives. And it really doesn't matter whether you go willingly or not. The basic balance of consequences remains the same: one life—yours, unfortunately—against six.

Suppose you tell the police officers that their analysis is too simple. There is another important branch on the decision tree. Killing you will set a bad precedent and lead to many other unfortunate outcomes. But the public officials have thought broadly and deeply about the consequences. Their operation is top-secret and won't be repeated. This is a special case because one of the six patients is a Nobel laureate scientist on the brink of discovering the cure for malaria. It seems the government officials have thought broadly. Your death could save millions of lives. They have also thought deeply: your death will be painless, and this will spare others slow, agonizing deaths. Clearly, if we consider only the first question, you should bid your loved ones farewell and head to the hospital.

This scenario reveals a profound flaw in the first question—and this flaw matters because the scenario is not as far-fetched as it first seems. Thinking about decisions and action in terms of consequences has a powerful intellectual, religious, political, and commonsense mandate. It underlies standard practices like cost-risk and cost-benefit analysis. But this approach to important decisions can also be dangerous and inhumane. During the last century, countless innocent people were murdered as Nazi and Communist leaders pursued their grand, perverted visions of what was best for society. Joseph Stalin once remarked, "A single death is a tragedy; a million deaths

40

is a statistic."[30] The first question risks turning each of us into a doormat for whatever benefits everyone else. It may elevate our lives in some ways, but it degrades us in others.

The first critical question resembles a blowtorch: it is a powerful and dangerous tool. This question is the right place to start thinking about gray area decisions, as a manager and as a human being, because it asks us to look at the whole picture in front of us, but we can't stop there. The question expresses a very important voice in the centuries-long conversation about human nature, power, and decision making, but it shouldn't be the only voice you listen to, when you face a gray area problem.

What other questions do you need? And, in the organ donor scenario, what is the deep flaw in the police officers' plan for achieving the best net, net consequences? The next chapter answers both of these questions.

3

What Are My Core Obligations?

If the police are about to take you to the operating room, there is something you can say, clearly and simply, that should change their minds and save your life. Tell them bluntly, "Killing me would be wrong. I am a human being, and you can't do this to me." That statement should stop the police in their tracks.

But what makes it so compelling? The answer is that it points to a fundamental principle—that it is wrong to directly take the life of an innocent human being—and it tells the police they have a duty to follow this principle. You are saying that, simply because you are a human being, the police have duties to you. And, because they are human beings, they can't violate these duties.

Notice that this statement doesn't say anything about calculating the net, net consequences. While it doesn't explicitly reject the first question, it does start fresh, and gives us an entirely new perspective on making hard decisions. This perspective is the second important voice in the great conversation, and the question it highlights is the second crucial question. The basic idea is that, to get really hard decisions right, you have to understand your basic duties as a human being. Hence, when you are trying to resolve a gray area problem, you have to develop an answer—for yourself—to the question of what your core human obligations require you to do and not do in the situation you face.

The organ transplant situation was a thought experiment, so consider for a moment what the perspective of basic human obligations shows us about one of the most important decisions in modern history. The United States fought the first nuclear war when it dropped atomic bombs on Hiroshima and Nagasaki in 1945. Two hundred thousand people died, some instantly and some after suffering burns, trauma, and radiation. Several days after the second bomb was dropped, President Truman told his secretary of war that he was having terrible headaches. When the secretary asked if the president was speaking literally or figuratively, Truman replied, "Both." He said he couldn't stand the thought of "killing all those children."[1] Then the president gave an order that no more atomic bombs could be used in the Pacific without his explicit approval.

Why did President Truman give this order and why was he having terrible headaches? Truman had fought in the trenches of Europe during World War I. He knew what the Allied soldiers and their families were suffering as the war in Asia ground on. He badly wanted to bring the long, devastating war to an end. But Truman also knew that thousands of children—utterly innocent infants and toddlers—had died in the atomic devastation. And he knew that this was wrong. These children were innocent, and killing innocent people for larger geopolitical agendas is wrong. In fact, we now view some versions of this logic as terrorism.

When President Truman said he couldn't stand the thought of killing children, he wasn't reporting his assessment of net, net consequences. He was thinking about a basic human duty and reacting, not just as president, but as a human being. Truman knew that killing innocent children was wrong, pure and simple, and didn't want to violate this basic human duty. But why did he think and feel this way? Why did Truman believe that adhering to this duty was the right way to make a momentous wartime decision—a decision that would be central to his legacy, as a president and as a person? And what does this way of thinking show us about the best way to make gray area decisions?

Our Core Human Obligations

Like all of the five questions, the second question works like a laser. It takes a wide range of complex, long-standing, fundamental ideas—about what counts as a good life, a good community, and a good decision—and concentrates them intensely and powerfully. The question distills and compresses religious insights, basic tenets of political philosophy, important ideas in evolutionary theory, as well as our everyday, instinctive reactions to pain, suffering, and death.

The short question—What are my core obligations?—focuses on a single, crucial humanist theme: that we have basic duties to each other simply because we are human beings. In other words, there is something profoundly important about our common human nature that creates, immediately and directly, certain fundamental obligations that we all owe to each other.[2]

The German philosopher Immanuel Kant expressed this idea beautifully. "Two things awe me most," he wrote, "the starry sky above me and the moral law within me."[3] The second voice in the great conversation says, in effect, that we have basic moral obligations that are as real as the sky above us. Meeting these obligations is the best way to make a good decision and live a good life. That is, of course, a strong and controversial claim, and it is easy to think of reasons to dispute it. So why have some of the most brilliant minds and most compassionate hearts believed that this way of thinking was a profound truth?

The clearest and oldest answer to this question appears in the great religious traditions. Islam, Judaism, Christianity, and Hinduism all teach that human beings are creatures of a special kind.[4] Some religions say we have souls or divine sparks; others teach that we are partly flesh and partly eternal spirit or the handiwork of a creator. Human beings, in other words, aren't just another rung on the ladder of evolution. For example, a basic principle of Catholic social teaching over the centuries is, "Being in the image of God, the human individual possesses the dignity of a person, who is not just something, but someone."[5]

It is only a short step from these religious views to thinking that we have strong, binding duties to each other—regardless of who we are, where we live, or the political system of our society. The Eastern traditions are very explicit about this.* For example, according to Confucius, all human beings have compelling duties to their families, their communities, and their governments. In the Western tradition, the ancient Greeks and Romans held similar views. In Cicero's classic essay "On Duties," he argues that each of us is bound by duties that originate in our human nature and the communities that surround us.[6] Seneca, another important Roman states- man and philosopher, wrote succinctly, "Man is a sacred thing for man."[7]

Even today, in the contemporary Western world, with its strong emphasis on individual rights, we continue to live in a world of duties. Many of these come with our roles in society: we have duties as parents, as children, as citizens, as employees, and as professionals. Even the people who are pre- occupied with asserting their rights cannot escape the world

---

*This book, at several points, makes a rough distinction between Western and Eastern ways of thinking and social practices. This is intended only to highlight broadly divergent tendencies. In reality, of course, neither the "West" nor the "East" was monolithic. Moreover, they had important elements in common, and the boundaries between them were blurred by extensive cross-fertilization of ideas. For example, the revival of interest in Aristotle during the twelfth and thirteenth centuries resulted from the extensive commentaries on his work by the Muslim philosopher Ibn Rushd, known also as Averroes. See Roger Arnaldez, *Averroes: a Rationalist in Islam* (Notre Dame, IN: University of Notre Dame Press, 2000).

of duties. This is because rights and duties are two sides of the same coin: If I have a right to my property, you have a duty to respect it. If you have a right to be told the truth, I have a duty to tell you the truth. In short, the idea that we have strong, binding duties to each other shapes our lives and institutions and suffuses our thinking.

Why is this the case? There is no definitive answer, but evolutionary theory suggests a fascinating and provocative explanation, one that we seem to be able to confirm in our everyday experience.[8] The basic idea is that, as a result of a genetic roll of the dice, some prehumans had a better sense of empathy than others. They could quickly grasp—perhaps relying on what some neurologists believe to be mirror neurons—what others were thinking and feeling. The prehumans with this capability did a better job of working together in groups to find and store food, protect their young, and fight predators. Hence, they were more likely to survive and pass their genetic disposition on to their children, who ultimately evolved into us.

That is speculation, of course, but daily life seems to confirm it. Think of explicit television coverage of child abuse or a violent crime. When we see these reports, we react viscerally. We feel—and seem to know with certainty—that what we have seen is wrong.[9] Something tells us, loud and clear, that human beings should never do these things to each other. And we can also feel there is something wrong with people who don't react this way. Some are odd birds who need a conceptual explanation of why these vicious actions are wrong. Their problem is that they are seeking "one reason too many."[10] Others seem completely unmoved, and we fear they are defective or depraved.

In short, the second question is a resounding chorus and not a solo performance. It pulls together a wide range of long-standing, profound insights—insights shared, not just by brilliant and compassionate thinkers, but by most of us in our everyday experience. The refrain is simple: we have basic duties to treat each other in certain ways. As human beings, these obligations should guide our decisions and our lives. The philosopher Kwame Anthony Appiah stated the principle with crystalline clarity. "No local loyalty," he wrote, "can ever justify forgetting that each human being has responsibilities to every other."[11]

The second great humanist question reflects this profound principle. It explains why it would be wrong for the police to make you an involuntary organ donor. It is why President Truman hated the thought of killing the Japanese children. The second question expresses a fundamental voice in the long conversation about what really matters in life, how the world really works, and the best way to make difficult, important decisions. That is why this question is so important for resolving gray area issues. It also means people who ignore this question when they face hard decisions are performing impressive feats of hubris, denial, or self-absorption.

The second question is vitally important, but is it practical? Imagine, for example, that you have been grappling with a gray area problem. You have approached it as a manager, working with others and developing the best information, analysis, and informed assessments you can reasonably get. Now you have to decide what to do. How will you know, specifically, what your core human obligations require in this situation? Where will you find the bright lines you cannot cross? To answer these questions, we will now turn to a manager who faced an extraordinarily challenging gray area problem and think through his situation in terms of his basic human duties.

The Practical Challenges

Imagine yourself in the position of Jim Mullen, the CEO of Biogen Idec. In 2004, Biogen was a small biotech company. After long years of effort, it had developed a new drug for treating multiple sclerosis, a disease that afflicts millions of people around the world and has unpredictable, frightening, sometimes severe symptoms. These range from fatigue, tingling sensations, weak muscles, and loss of balance to seizures, depression, cognitive decline, and, in very severe cases, death.

Biogen's new product, called Tysabri, seemed to be a major step forward in treating MS. As one patient put it, "I got better. Not miraculous jump up and run a race better, but I did walk to the duck pond with my two five-year-old boys. I stood up long enough to cook dinner and I smiled more often. That is what hope does. That is what Tysabri does for me."[12]

Because Tysabri proved so effective during the first year of clinical trials, the Food and Drug Administration approved Biogen's request to introduce the drug before the full clinical trials were complete. The company raced to get Tysabri to market. In a single year, Biogen built two new manufacturing facilities, arranged for third-party payments, reorganized its sales force, completed the final phase of research for the FDA, and had seven thousand patients taking Tysabri. Another fifteen thousand patients were waiting for their managed care providers to approve it. Biogen Idec's stock reached a record high.

On a Friday morning in February, Jim Mullen held a town hall meeting for Biogen Idec employees to thank them for their hard work and congratulate them on all they had accomplished. When he got back to his office, he found a voice mail message from the executive responsible for product safety. It said, "Jim, we need to talk. Call me immediately." Mullen knew this was bad news. He quickly learned that a patient in the Tysabri clinical trial had died of progressive multifocal leukoencephalopathy (PML), an extremely rare brain infection, and another patient, who seemed to have the same illness, was in critical condition. This was a very rare infection. One incident might have been an isolated event, but two pointed toward Tysabri as a contributing factor.

We will return to Mullen's problem and the decisions he made in several of the following chapters, because they illustrate important ideas and themes. For now, however, notice what this situation reveals about the challenges of meeting your basic human obligations when you face a gray area problem.

Mullen's situation raised a long series of questions about his duties. The first was how to deal with the multiplicity of duties he had. The PML problem involved his legal duties to current patients, prospective patients, the doctors and nurses treating them, government regulators in many countries, and various groups of shareholders. Mullen also had a parallel set of duties—ethical duties—to each of these parties. And, if we look closely, we find that none of these legal and ethical duties was simple.

For example, what were Mullen's duties to patients taking Tysabri? Was he obligated, legally or ethically, to immediately inform their doctors about the PML cases? Did he have a duty to inform the patients right away? Or did he have an obligation to first get to the root of the problem? Perhaps his duty was to withdraw Tysabri immediately. Or did patients have the right to decide whether to keep taking the drug and run the risk of PML, once they had been informed about the problem?

Mullen's problem with a multiplicity of duties is hardly unique. Put the Tysabri case aside for a moment and think about the many rights that people frequently assert. Lists of these rights go on and on. One list included, "A right to life, a right to choose; a right to vote, to work, to strike; a right to one phone call, to dissolve parliament, to operate a forklift, to asylum, to equal treatment before the law, to feel proud of what one has done; a right to exist, to sentence an offender to death, to launch a nuclear first strike, to castle kingside, to a distinct genetic identity; a right to believe one's eyes, to pronounce the couple husband and wife, to be left alone, to go to hell in one's own way."[13] All of these rights create duties for others. Like insects in a rain forest, duties and duty-generating rights swarm all around us.

The further complication is that these duties come in all different forms. Some are legal and regulatory; some are familiar, others esoteric; some seem inconsequential, and others shape our lives. So do some duties or types of duty have priority over others? And what about situations in which duties conflict? An everyday example is the conflict between telling the truth and being kind to our friends. In short, the multiplicity of duties creates serious practical problems. How do you know what your duties are in a particular situation? How do you prioritize your duties? And what do you do when one duty contradicts another? Another layer of difficulty is that we shouldn't assume we can sort out our duties in a sensible or rational way. Growing up, most of us learned a long list of do's and don'ts—obey your parents, keep your room clean, be respectful, and so on—and we learned from parents and other authority figures. Quite often, their strong voices echo inside us, telling us unconsciously what we should and shouldn't do and generating a wide range of feelings.

Even worse, there is very strong evidence that, even when we are fully aware of our duties, internal and external forces often keep us from doing what we know we should do. A famous example involved students at Princeton Theological Seminary. They attended a lecture on the biblical parable of the Good Samaritan. By design, the lecture ran overtime, so the students were late for their next class. On their way, they passed a man—an accomplice in the experiment—who was slumped in a doorway, groaning and coughing. Only ten of the sixty-three students were Good Samaritans and stopped to help him.[14] The others went directly to class.

A century ago, the American psychologist William James wrote, "The trail of the human serpent is over everything."[15] James stated what contemporary social science has repeatedly and unambiguously confirmed: in countless, often unseen ways, our interests, biases, and blind spots shape and often distort what we firmly believe to be clear, objective thinking about the consequences of our actions, as we saw in the last chapter, and about our duties.

The Tysabri case forces us to ask what the second question really means in practice. What do you do when you are trying to take your basic obligations seriously, but duties assail you on every side? And how can you grasp, with clarity and without bias and distortion, what your core human obligations really are?

Practical Guidance: Awaken Your Moral Imagination

There is a time-tested way to answer this question. It is to rely on what has long been called our "moral imagination." This section will explain what our moral imagination is, why it is so important, and how it can help us with gray area problems. But, before you can use your moral imagination, you have to take two preliminary steps. Each involves clearing your head of a familiar, plausible, but fundamentally inadequate answer to the second question. Both of these answers purport to tell you what your core obligations are, and both can be seriously misleading.

Look Past the Economics

The first piece of practical guidance says that, when you face a gray area issue, you have to look hard at the economics of the situation and you also have to look past the economics. In other words, running the numbers and grasping what they tell you is important, but not enough. You also have to put aside a specific piece of conventional wisdom.

This is the mistaken view that, if you are a business manager, your central or exclusive duty is to earn profits, maximize returns, create shareholder value, or just make money. Obviously, most companies need to earn strong profits, and organizations of all kinds need to pay close attention to their finances. And their managers need to be skilled at doing this. That is why the basic guidance in this book says you should first approach gray area issues *like a manager.* This means really understanding the economic realities. If you don't do this, for gray area and routine decisions, you will make bad decisions, weaken your organization, and likely limit your career prospects.

But, when you face gray area problems, you have to resolve them *as a human being.* In these situations, you have to look beyond the economics, if you want to understand and meet your basic human obligations.

For example, should Jim Mullen have ignored the long tradition of serious thought about what we owe each other as human beings and instead tried to resolve the Tysabri crisis in whatever way would maximize shareholder returns? Should he have paid attention to the benefits and risks of the drug for MS patients only to the extent they affected Biogen's bottom line? By the same token, should managers responsible for layoffs look solely at the economics? Should they put aside the hard, sometimes devastating, impact layoffs have on employees and instead view their workers as soft-tissue assets that should be valued, deployed, maintained, depreciated, and sometimes scrapped, just like machinery?

From a historical perspective, the idea that managers in organizations have a single, dominant duty—to maximize economic returns—is a striking development. Somehow, a theoretical assumption—widely used in one cluster of academic specialties: economics, finance, econometric modeling, and the like—became transformed, primarily in the United States near the end of the twentieth century, into a supreme decision principle. From a humanist perspective, this notion is a stunning development. No list of basic human duties, religious or secular, has ever included an overriding requirement to make large amounts of money for certain groups. If anything, the great traditions of thought strongly discourage preoccupation with wealth and riches.

But perhaps you have no choice. Aren't business managers, at least those working in the Anglo-American system of capitalism, obligated by law to maximize shareholder returns? The answer to this question is no, and this is why it is important, when you face a gray area decision, to look beyond the economics of the situation. Nothing in American corporate law says that business managers have an open-ended, always-on obligation to maximize the financial interests of shareholders.[16] What the law actually says is quite different: the legal duty of managers is to serve the interests of the shareholders and the corporation. That is a very broad mandate, and the law gives managers and executives a good deal of flexibility in pursuing it.[17]

A recent exchange between Tim Cook, the CEO of Apple, and an activist shareholder dramatized the actual legal reality. The shareholder asked Cook about the company's renewable energy program and told him that Apple should only pursue these efforts if they were profitable. In a rare display of anger, Cook replied that there were many things Apple did because they were right and just. "When we work on making our devices accessible by the blind," he said, "I don't consider the bloody ROI." Then he added, "If you want me to do things only for ROI reasons, you should get out of this stock."[18]

In the United States, the business judgment rule gives executives and boards of directors wide discretion in setting the objectives companies pursue—as long as their motives aren't tainted by conflicts of interest and as long as they make reasonable efforts to make informed decisions. In addition, thirty states have passed laws that explicitly authorize companies to consider the interests of parties other than shareholders. The American Law Institute has stated that managers have discretion to sacrifice profits to avoid conduct that may "unethically" harm employees, suppliers, communities, and other parties.[19]

The rationale for profit maximization is basically pragmatic. It is a simple, clear, and useful criterion—for routine decisions in businesses operating in competitive markets and with sound legal systems. In these circumstances, thinking in terms of long-term profit and returns is an important way of putting society's resources to their best uses. In competitive markets, strong profits can be critical to survival and success. But the important obligation to earn strong returns doesn't override or replace your fundamental duties as a human being. And managers have to be careful that they don't use their economic obligations as excuses for ignoring these duties. This is why, when you face a gray area issue and want to understand your basic duties, you need to look hard at the economics and also look beyond the economics.

Look Past the Stakeholders

What about thinking in terms of duties to stakeholders? This is the conventional alternative to a sharp focus on returns to shareholders. This view says that, when you make important decisions, you should be responsive to the interests of outside groups, and not just shareholders.[20] Typically, these groups are an organization's customers or clients, employees, suppliers, government regulators, and the communities where the organization operates.

Is stakeholder analysis the right way for managers to grasp their basic duties? The answer is a qualified no. The stakeholder view is valuable and important. It is a strong, practical antidote to narrow preoccupation with profits. It tells managers to think carefully, responsibly, and strategically about all the groups with a stake in what they do. It also pushes managers to develop sound plans for managing relationships with these groups. But stakeholder analysis has two serious problems.

First, it is too general. Telling you to pay attention to your duties to stakeholders isn't telling you very much. It doesn't tell you which groups have the highest priority or what duties managers and companies have to these high-priority groups. Stakeholder analysis can point you in the right direction—it says to take a hard look at important outside groups, understand their interests, their power, and your responsibilities to them—but it doesn't tell you what stakes or whose stakes really matter.

The second problem is that, because stakeholder analysis is general, it creates a serious temptation: to focus on larger, established, familiar groups, especially if they have political or economic clout. This isn't the textbook approach to stakeholder analysis, but it is a real-world hazard. The risk was encapsulated in a classic line from the film *Casablanca*: "Round up the usual suspects."[21] And Aaron Feuerstein may have fallen into this trap. He focused so heavily on the immediate interests of visible, familiar stakeholders, with whom he had a long working relationship, that he failed to consider his longer-term duties to them. He took care of the current workforce at Malden Mills, but only on a short-term basis. No one represented the many workers—at Malden Mills, elsewhere in the United States, and even around the world— who might have benefited, in the long run, if Feuerstein had been willing to rethink and restructure Malden Mills and thereby provide sustainable jobs for years to come.

By focusing on established groups, managers may overlook long-term opportunities. They can also miss serious duties to groups that have been marginalized or lack political clout. And they are more likely to be attentive to groups that want to preserve the past rather than shape the future. The title of a recent book—*The Future and Its Enemies*—highlights this problem. Its basic question is: Who represents the future? Who represents the interests of groups that are tiny or yet to form?[22] Established industries and companies have many friends in the political capitals of the world; new entrepreneurial companies usually don't.[23]

Fortunately, Jim Mullen avoided the hazards of stakeholder analysis. Many different groups had a stake in his decisions about Tysabri. So should Mullen have "rounded up the usual suspects" and developed a plan that served the interests of his company's shareholders, its employees, local communities, patients, doctors, and regulatory agencies in many countries? Or should he have focused sharply on his duties to a single group, the patients now taking Tysabri? Mullen didn't ignore Biogen's stakeholder groups, but he focused sharply on the company's clear, fundamental human duty to Tysabri patients. This duty dominated obligations to other groups with a stake of some sort in his company.

Awaken Your Moral Imagination

When you face a particular gray area problem, how do you know what your core human obligations are? And how do you figure out what they mean in this particular situation? The answer, in short, is that you have to rely on your moral imagination.

The idea of a moral imagination is unfamiliar nowadays, but it has a long and impressive legacy. In its simplest form, your moral imagination is a kind of voice. In certain situations, it tells you, sometimes urgently, that something is seriously wrong, you can't ignore it, and you have to act. President Truman was exercising his moral imagination when he said, "I can't stand the thought of killing all those kids" and then restricted further use of the atomic bomb.

To see what moral imagination means in concrete terms, recall the gray area decision described in the first chapter, involving the long-term employee whose work had slipped badly. This situation is a disguised version of actual events, so I will call the employee Kathy Thompson and her boss Alisha Wilson. The managers Wilson worked with and supervised were really frustrated with Thompson. Most of them wanted to hand the situation off to HR, with the expectation that

Thompson would be terminated. Wilson was deeply reluctant to do this. She felt that the assistant was struggling with serious physical or emotional problems. At one point, Wilson said, "I was really afraid Kathy could end up living on the street."

When Wilson made that statement, she was expressing what her moral imagination had told her. Wilson was saying that she and her management team, who had worked with Thompson for years, owed her special concern and special treatment. Wilson believed and felt that they had a serious obligation, as human beings, to do more than put Thompson into the HR system for termination and get her a severance payment and a letter of reference.

More than two centuries ago, the British statesman, historian, and philosopher Edmund Burke gave the classic definition of the moral imagination: it is a reaction to a situation that "the heart owns and the understanding ratifies."[24] Burke's words exactly describe Alisha Wilson's reaction to Kathy Thompson's situation. It was a fusion of feeling and thinking, of heart and mind. Wilson's heart—her instinctive reaction as a human being—told her she had serious responsibility for another person's welfare. She saw and feared the prospect of Thompson "living on the streets." When Wilson thought about this, she understood it was a real possibility, because her assistant's problem seemed so profound. Wilson thought that she and the managers who worked for her had a special obligation, as human beings, to Thompson, who was not only their long-term employee, but also a friend. In Burke's words, Wilson's understanding ratified what her heart owned.

What kinds of situations trigger our moral imagination? There is no comprehensive answer to this question but, in many cases, like those involving Alisha Wilson and Jim Mullen, two basic human obligations are at stake.

The first centers on the basic human right to live without needless danger, pain, and suffering. The primacy of this right is clear. At bottom, its rationale has nothing to do with political documents or philosophical arguments. Instead, it rests on a humanist perspective—that is, on a broad and empathic understanding of human experience that tells us certain things are wrong and we are bound to try hard to keep them from happening to our fellow human beings. What are these things? Stuart Hampshire, an important, contemporary moral philosopher, wrote, "There is nothing mysterious or 'subjective' or culture-bound in the great evils of human experience, re-affirmed in every age and in every written history and in every tragedy and fiction: murder and the destruction of life, imprisonment, enslavement, starvation, poverty, physical pain and torture, homelessness, friendlessness. That these great evils are to be averted is the constant presupposition of moral arguments at all times and in all places . . . "[25] Put differently, we all have a fundamental right not to have our lives taken or wrecked. This means managers have a profound human duty not to seriously impair or risk the lives of others.

The other frequent trigger of our moral imagination involves situations in which people are not being treated with the respect and dignity that, as human beings, they deserve.[26] This obligation, as we have seen, has deep roots in religious traditions around the world. It is also embedded in the basic idea of democracy: the idea that we all count, and we all count the same.

Neither of these two deep obligations can be specified precisely or completely. There is no bulletproof philosophical argument that mandates our belief in them. But neither fact gives managers permission to ignore these duties or replace them with something else, like the economics of their organizations. In fact, because these two basic human duties are open-ended, managers have to work harder and think more carefully about what they require in particular situations.

The Tysabri situation shows the importance of making this effort. Mullen's decision, as we have seen, would determine which of his fellow human beings got medicine they really needed and when they would get it. He was deciding who suffers and who might live or die. This gave Mullen a clear, overriding duty to focus intently on patient health. This duty trumped any obligations to Biogen Idec's shareholders or to any other stakeholder group. The patients on Tysabri also had a right to be treated with dignity and respect. This meant Mullen and Biogen Idec had a duty to tell them the truth, as best he and his company could discern it, about the benefits and risks of Tysabri.

Attack the Obstacles

It is easy to say, "Rely on your moral imagination." In practice, however, this may not happen spontaneously and, when you are under real pressure, it may not happen at all. Hence, process really matters—just as it does when you are assessing the net, net consequences. To awaken your moral imagination, you have to take two steps. The first is recognizing the obstacles to doing this. The second is working actively, with others and on your own, to grasp what your moral imagination is telling you.

What are the obstacles and how serious are they? The answer comes from a surprising individual: the great classical economist Adam Smith. Although he is best known for articulating certain fundamental economic principles, like the "invisible hand" of the market, Smith was actually a humanist thinker. His most famous book is the economics treatise, *The Wealth of Nations*, but the truest statement of Smith's personal philosophy was a study of human psychology called *The Theory of Moral Sentiments*.[27]

In one chapter, Smith discusses how people typically react to news about far-off catastrophes. What is striking is how precisely his account, written more than two hundred years ago, describes how we react today, when a massive human tragedy occurs somewhere in the world. Smith imagines an earthquake that kills everyone in China. Then he sketches the immediate reaction of someone in Europe. This person, "would, I imagine, first of all, express very strongly his sorrow for the misfortune of that unhappy people, he would make many melancholy deliberations upon the precariousness of human life, and the vanity of all the labours of man, which could thus be annihilated in a moment."[28]

This reaction, Smith tells us, lasts for several minutes, but what does our empathic European do next? Smith writes, "When all this fine philosophy was over, when all these humane sentiments had been once fairly expressed, he would pursue his business or his pleasure, take his repose or his diversion, with the same ease and tranquility, as if no such accident had happened."[29] What Adam Smith, an astute observer of the human condition, shows us is all too familiar: the moral imagination welling up in sympathy with the Chinese people and then quickly subsiding.

What makes our moral imaginations fragile or fleeting? One factor, for managers, is simply busyness. Managers work, in effect, on an endless conveyor belt that brings them problem after problem. Some are big, some small, many are messy and complex, and most have to be handled expeditiously—so you can get to the next problem or issue. Organizational routines are another obstacle: often, we don't really think and instead just do whatever is familiar, reinforced, and rewarded. In Kathy Thompson's situation, the standard operating procedure was sending her file to HR.

Another obstacle, a surprising one, is success. Years ago, an executive looked back on his career in New York City. When he started out, his pay was low and he took the bus to work. Later, he moved to the suburbs and drove. At the pinnacle of his career, he rode to work in a limousine and took an executive elevator to a corner office atop a skyscraper. Every promotion, he later realized, separated him further from the life experience of many other people. Each step up made him a more powerful and successful man and also more of a bubble child.

Unfortunately, the barriers to our moral imagination run even deeper. They include, not just busyness, routines, and anesthetizing success, but human nature itself. We evolved as tribal creatures. We draw lines between "us and them," between insiders and outsiders, often on the flimsiest grounds. And we instinctively take care of our own. As a result, our moral imaginations work with blinders on. E. O. Wilson, one of the most influential biologists of recent decades, has written, "Our bloody nature, it can now be argued in the context of modern biology, is ingrained because group-versus-group was a principal driving force that made us what we are."[30] This tendency skews our moral imaginations, and it may be why Adam Smith's imaginary European quickly turned his attention from the Chinese calamity.

Ask What Is Hateful

So how do you deal with all these obstacles, if you are facing a hard gray area decision and don't want to bypass your basic human obligations? The challenge is to see yourself as "the other"—as one of the outsiders or victims, and not as the insider, the decision maker, the dominant party. And the harder challenge is to grasp and feel the experience of "the other" in a way that vividly highlights your core obligations as a human being.

A practical way to do this is by spending a few moments trying to answer a very old question. It was articulated by Hillel the Elder, the ancient Hebrew philosopher and theologian. He spoke with a man who was willing to convert to Judaism, but only on one condition: that Hillel could explain the entire Torah to him, during the time that Hillel could stand on one foot. Hillel met the challenge easily. He simply said, "That which is hateful unto you, do not do to your neighbor. That is the whole Torah. The rest is commentary. Go and study it."[31]

The striking word here is "hateful." Hillel is asking us to pay attention to what we would really care about, deeply and urgently, if we were in another person's situation. In practice, this means finding ways to ask yourself and others what you would be thinking and feeling if you were among the people hit hardest by the decision you might make. Try to imagine how you would react if your parents or children or some other loved ones were in this vulnerable position? What if *you* were the victim of MS or PML? What would you be feeling and thinking? What would you urgently want? What if one of your children or your parents or your partner had MS? Or might get PML? What basic duties do you think Jim Mullen and his company would have to you or to your loved ones?

The familiar version of Hillel's guidance is the Golden Rule: "Do unto others as you would have them do unto you."[32] In the West, most people view this precept as a teaching of Christian religion, which relegates it to occasional sermons in certain houses of worship. But that view misses the full force of the question Hillel wants us to ask. The Golden Rule isn't simply a precept of Christianity. Versions of it appear in almost every major religion. Some philosophers have argued that the Golden Rule is part of the foundation of important moral theories.[33] And it is easy to hear it echoed in everyday, practical moral guidance—like the Native American recommendation to "Walk a mile in the other person's shoes."

Dismissing the Golden Rule as Sunday sermonizing, rather than seeing it as an almost universal humanist insight, is a serious mistake. The moral imagination is basically a secular version of it. And Hillel's version—which asks what we would find hateful—has a sharp edge. This question has endured for two millennia because it prods our dormant moral imaginations. It pushes us to think imaginatively and sympathetically about the experiences of others as a way of understanding what our core human obligations require in a particular situation.

Asking this question is valuable, but it is still hard to awaken your moral imagination on your own. This is another reason why process—working with and through others, in the right ways—is so important. This is why it is particularly valuable for managers and teams working on gray area problems to find ways to escape their organizational bubbles and hear directly from people whose livelihoods and lives will be affected by their decision or from people who can represent their experience in direct, concrete, forceful ways. Unless you find a way to do this, you may unwittingly buy into Joseph Stalin's observation, mentioned in the last chapter, and harden yourself to individual hardships and tragedies by focusing on statistical aggregates.

Another approach is to ask someone to play the role of the outsider and victim and do so as vividly and persuasively as they can, so everyone else hears at least some version of the urgent, basic needs of the people a gray area decision will affect. This approach is sometimes described as making sure there is a "barbarian" at every meeting—someone who will speak awkward truths, clearly and urgently.[34] In the situation involving Kathy Thompson, Alisha Wilson played this role herself, when she told the managers working for her that she was afraid that Thompson could be hit so hard by losing her job that she might end up living on the street.

All these tactics are ways of taking the second question seriously. They are ways of looking beyond the economics, the shareholders, and the stakeholders and working hard to awaken your moral imagination. The second question tells us, in effect: Don't think your position in society or in an organization exempts you from basic human duties. Don't get trapped in your own interests, experiences, judgments, and ways of seeing the world. Do everything you can to escape from your egocentric prison. Try hard, on your own and with others, to imagine how you would feel and what you would really want and need, if you were actually that person.

A Good Start

We have now looked at two fundamental humanist questions, one focused on consequences and the other on duties, and at practical guidelines for using them. How much do they help us with gray area problems? The answer is that we have made real progress—and we also have more work to do.

We now have the basics of a useful framework. The first two questions say, in effect, don't plunge ahead when you face gray area problems. Instead, take time, work with others, and think for yourself. Try hard to grasp the full consequences of the options in front of you. And spend some time thinking hard, imaginatively, and concretely about your basic duties as a human being.

To see how useful these questions are, look for a moment at how they cut to critical trade-offs on really difficult issues. For example, should governments monitor private phone calls and internet communication? Supporters of monitoring argue in terms of consequences: they want to prevent horrific terrorist acts. Opponents of monitoring argue in terms of rights, specifically the right to privacy. The gun-control debate in the United States breaks down on the same lines. Advocates of greater control emphasize the consequences for innocent people when the wrong people get weapons. Their opponents argue for the rights of law-abiding citizens under the Constitution.

The first two questions cut to the core of great historical decisions, like President Truman's decisions about using the atomic bomb. His terrible trade-off was between saving the lives of Allied soldiers by dropping the two atomic bombs and sacrificing the lives of innocent children. Historians continue to debate whether Truman got the trade-off right. Perhaps the war was about to end and no atomic bombs were needed. Perhaps one bomb would have led to the Japanese surrender. In any event, the first two questions in the humanist framework reveal the fundamental features of Truman's situation.

These examples all show how the first two humanist questions can cut through complex and controversial issues and reveal basic trade-offs in gray area situations. Used together, the two questions can do even more—because sometimes they work as a funnel. That is, they can help us reduce the range of options we really need to consider, by excluding some options with undesirable consequences and others that violate basic duties.[35]

But, in gray areas, we need more than clarity about trade-offs. We also need to do more than eliminate some options. The critical question is, which option or plan of action should we pursue? And we need a plan that will work—that will move a team, a department, or an entire organization through a gray area, responsibly and successfully. This means taking a pragmatic perspective. To understand what this pragmatic perspective really is, we will now turn to another timeless idea and another important—and surprising—humanist thinker, Niccolò Machiavelli.

4

What Will Work in the World as It Is?

Georges Frederic Doriot was an extraordinary individual. He was French by birth, became an American citizen, taught at Harvard Business School, served as a Brigadier General in the US Army during World War II and worked on military planning, and then founded the American Research and Development Corporation. This was the first important American venture capital firm, and Doriot is widely regarded as "the father of venture capital."[1] He was also known for his practical wisdom. For example, Doriot often gave managers this advice: if you have to choose between a great strategy with a good action plan and a good strategy with a great action plan, you should pick the second option.[2]

In short, what mattered for Doriot was what worked. "Without actions," he once said, "the world would still be an idea."[3] This way of thinking is the basic premise of the third crucial question. It asks: What will work in the world as it is? And that is, of course, an utterly unsurprising question for a manager—except for the phrase at the end, "in the world as it is." Those are the words of Niccolò Machiavelli. They were his way of saying that leaders who faced hard decisions had to be, above all, realistic and pragmatic and not let idealistic notions distort their thinking.

Machiavelli can seem like a very odd choice for a humanist perspective on hard decisions. He was, indeed, a humanist, but his ideas are widely reviled. Machiavelli lived in Florence during the late Renaissance and served the Medici as a senior government official, so he understood politics and leadership from the inside. He was also a prolific writer and is best known for his handbook of political leadership, *The Prince*, which is still widely read and discussed—and condemned.

Machiavelli is also known, fairly or unfairly, for saying that the ends justify the means and believing that the means could be deceit, treachery, a poisoned chalice, or a stiletto between the ribs. The British historian Thomas Babington Macaulay began his account of Machiavelli's thinking with the warning, "We doubt whether any name in literary history be so generally odious as that of the man whose character and writings we now propose to consider."[4]

So should Machiavelli be mentioned with John Stuart Mill, Confucius, Aristotle, and Thomas Jefferson? How can a reprobate of historic proportions serve as a guide to effective and responsible decisions? These questions seem serious—until we ask something else: Would we know Machiavelli's name today, if all he said was that you can get ahead in life by being sleazy? This observation hardly merits five hundred years of renown. All the ancients—Greek, Roman, and Chinese—understood that power-hungry, savvy, unscrupulous people could do quite well in life. Almost all of us think we know a few people who succeeded because they were fairly smart, worked reasonably hard, had some luck, and were willing to cut corners or worse.

Machiavelli must be telling us something more. That would explain why his guidance endured for centuries. So what does his voice contribute to the long conversation about power, decision making, and responsibility? And what advice does he have for managers working on gray area problems?

The World as It Is

The basic answer to this question is that Machiavelli believed that, if you have serious responsibilities, you must avoid the trap of seeing the world as you want it to be. You have to keep your eyes wide open and see the world as it is. That means Machiavelli would discourage you from relying on the guidance in the last two chapters because it is optimistic and naive.[5] The first question asks us to do what is best for everyone. The second says to focus sharply on our basic duties. In a virtuous, stable, predictable world, those sentiments would be fine, but that isn't our world.

The world we live in, as Machiavelli sees it, has three features. First, it is unpredictable. Sound plans can turn out badly, and bad plans sometimes work. Second, the world is often a very tough place. Much of what happens is simply outside our control. Leaders often have few degrees of freedom, limited resources, and can't avoid hard, sometimes painful choices. Third, the world as it is can be hazardous and dangerous, because it is heavily shaped by individuals and groups pursuing their own interests, sometimes clumsily and sometimes with sharply honed strategic skills. In the world as it is, Machiavelli warned, "Any man who under all conditions insists on making it his business to be good will surely be destroyed among so many who are not good."[6]

This is an ominous picture, yet it describes situations most managers have experienced. Several years ago, for example, a twenty-seven-year-old manager at an online retailer was under pressure from her bosses to change a performance evaluation she was about to submit for someone on her staff. The manager, Becky Friedman, was responsible for a small, highly productive group of fourteen people who handled online clothing sales. The team was under intense performance pressure, but one individual, Terry Fletcher, wasn't doing his part.

Fletcher had been hired when the company was growing fast and its prospects seemed strong. He was a good friend of several senior executives and was teaching scuba diving to some of them. Fletcher had done badly in his hiring interviews, but his connections got him a job anyway. Friedman's predecessor had given him scores of 3.5 on the company's five-point performance scale. This supposedly meant he was a solid performer, but it probably meant his boss was playing it safe.

When Friedman took over, she gave Fletcher several opportunities to develop his skills and contribute to her unit, but nothing came of them. Most of the other team members had strong software skills or in-depth industry experience, and there was no quick way for Fletcher to acquire either.

Friedman decided to give Fletcher the performance rating she thought he deserved. This was a 2.5. And she planned to put him on a PIP, a so-called performance improvement plan. Many companies use PIPs, but Friedman's company used it as a greased chute for getting rid of employees. Fletcher's work would be scrutinized intensely for the next six months. If he made a single mistake during this period, he would be fired. A 2.5 rating accompanied by a PIP was basically an organizational death sentence.

When they heard about Friedman's tentative decision, two of the company's vice presidents paid her a visit. She later reported that they asked, "What's going on?" and "Are you sure about this rating, since Fletcher's been getting 3.5s?" and "Do you really know what you're doing?" When Friedman told them Fletcher simply wasn't qualified for the job, they suggested the real problem might be her management skills and not his background. After the meeting, Friedman had no doubt about the high-stakes politics of her situation.

She also had other concerns. Fletcher was fifteen years older than her, which made their whole relationship awkward. She later said, "Fletcher just didn't seem well balanced. He had a lot of things in his life that weren't good." She knew he had a rifle in his car because he sometimes went target shooting after work and on weekends. For Friedman, the only positive factor was that Fletcher had given himself a 3.0 performance rating, so he knew he wasn't doing well.

Friedman's situation wouldn't surprise Machiavelli. Her company described itself as a meritocracy with high performance standards and a sharp focus on customer needs. This is what Friedman was told, and what she hoped for, when she joined the company. Instead, she found that several powerful people in the organization took care of themselves and their pals, tried hard to settle scores, and pressured other employees to play these games. As a result, even though Friedman wanted to give Fletcher the rating he deserved, she knew that political realities pointed her in the opposite direction.

In essence, the third question for managers facing gray area issues asks if they recognize that the world in which they live and work is unpredictable, constrained, and skewed by individuals and groups serving their own interests. The question asks managers if they are prepared to do what is necessary in this world—to serve the interests of people who depend on them and also protect themselves and advance their own objectives.

Human Nature, Realism, and Pragmatism

The third question, like the first two, can easily be abused or trivialized. As we will see, the abuse is interpreting the question as a mandate for pursuing simpleminded, short-term self-interest. The question can be trivialized by reducing it to any of the familiar sayings that simply advocate suspicion and distrust. Mark Twain, for example, wrote that, "Everyone is a moon, and has a dark side which he never shows to any-body."[7] Two millennia earlier, the Roman philosopher, con-sul, and lawyer Marcus Tullius Cicero advised, "Trust no one unless you have eaten much salt with him."[8] Another venera-ble adage, attributed to a wide range of writers, says, "Believe none of what you hear, and only half of what you see."[9] These are sensible sayings, but they don't communicate what the third question is asking you to think about. To grasp this, you need to understand the deeper levels of meaning in the pragmatic perspective.

The third question has deep roots in both Western and Eastern traditions of thought. In fact, the intellectual roots of this perspective may extend even further than the ideas of the net, net consequences and basic human duties. At bottom, the question is asking what you think about human nature: Are human beings are predominantly good or predominantly evil?

Machiavelli wrote nothing about biology or evolution, but the third question—at its deepest level—is consistent with the findings of these two sciences. As we have seen, the human creature may have evolved with some cooperative instincts, and these may have enabled certain groups to survive, but we are also deeply self-interested. The poet Alfred Tennyson captured this in the famous phrase, "nature, red in tooth and claw."[10] In other words, we may be natural-born cooperators, but we are also natural-born killers. All societies confront the problem of alpha males. According to anthropologists, these are primates or human creatures driven to acquire, aggran-dize, dominate, and conquer. A kindred problem is the hard-wired tendency, in almost all humans, to pursue and protect their own interests.[11]

At another deep level, Machiavelli's ideas resonate with the great religious traditions, and in a surprising way. *The Prince*, his best-known work, is essentially godless. It barely mentions sin, divine rule, or redemption. And yet Machiavelli's view of human nature is wholly consistent with long-standing religious perspectives on human nature, which show us as malleable, easily corruptible creatures.

At the beginning of the Old Testament, for example, Adam and Eve violate God's rules and eat the forbidden fruit. Cain, one of their sons, proceeds to betray, deceive, and kill his brother Abel. Then book after book of the Bible describes the foibles, perversities, treacheries, and cruelties of individuals and groups, of ordinary people and exalted rulers—despite the clear edicts and harsh sanctions of an all-powerful and all-seeing God. Other religious traditions give us a similar view. For example, one account of ancient Hindu traditions says, "The human condition is thus an ongoing experience of fragmentation, isolation, and loneliness. Consequently, our social worlds are riddled with crime and hostile conflict."[12]

Ancient secular texts also give us a similar view of our fellow human beings—and ourselves. Perhaps the best-known classical Chinese guide to effective leadership is *The Art of War*, written in roughly 500 BC. Its author, Sun Tzu, was a philosopher, so he thought deeply about basic questions, but he was also a general and understood the practical challenges of leadership. Sun Tzu wrote to advise other military leaders, but men and women in many other walks of life, in Asia and in the West, have turned to him for practical advice.

Sun Tzu saw the world as a battlefield, where success demands foresight, strategy, cunning, adaptability, and psychological acuity. So he gives advice that Machiavelli would endorse and that the third question emphasizes.[13] He tells his readers, for example:

> Be extremely subtle, even to the point of formless-
> ness. Be extremely mysterious, even to the point
> of soundlessness. Thereby you can be the direc-
> tor of the opponent's fate. All warfare is based on
> deception. Hence, when we are able to attack, we
> must seem unable; when using our forces, we must
> appear inactive; when we are near, we must make
> the enemy believe we are far away; when far away,
> we must make him believe we are near ... O divine
> art of subtlety and secrecy![14]

We see a similar perspective if we look at the practical-minded thinkers in our modern era who tried to devise the best forms of government. They advocate transparency, checks and balances, countervailing power, and other ways of restraining what governments, rulers, and politicians do. In the spirit of Machiavellian realism, they tried to design governments that would protect us from ourselves and from our governments. They weren't trying, naively, to suppress self-interest; all they hoped to do was channel it constructively. Giambattista Vico, the seventeenth-century Italian political philosopher and historian, wrote: "Legislation considers man as he is in order to turn him to good uses in human society. Out of ferocity, avarice and ambition, the three vices which run throughout the human race, it creates the military, mer-chant, and governing classes, and thus the strength, riches and wisdom of commonwealths. Out of these three great vices, which could certainly destroy all mankind on the face of the earth, it makes civil happiness."[15]

A deep current of thought running through contemporary biological science, the great religious and political traditions, and Machiavelli's worldview says, in effect: Look closely at human nature, see it for what it is, and don't kid yourself. Some of the people around you are self-interested, coldly rational, and strategic. They are in the game for themselves and themselves alone, and they are dangerous because they know how to play the game. Then there are others, who are also pursuing their self-interest, but in shortsighted, ham-fisted, ineffective ways. Finally, there are people who have more or less sound characters and try to do what seems right and sensible. All these types of individuals—the brilliantly devious, the inept and confused, and the mostly solid citizens—are out there, all around us. They are continuously acting, reacting, vying, jostling, maneuvering, scheming, and colliding. That is the world as it is.

Perhaps the deepest and most challenging theme in all of Machiavelli's thinking is the idea that the turbulence, uncertainty, and danger all around us create special *ethical* responsibilities for men and women who have to make hard decisions in organizations. They have to confront the hard realities of human nature head-on. If they don't, they are much more likely to fail and hurt everyone who depends on them.

The philosopher Stuart Hampshire stated this idea succinctly and powerfully. "The safety of the morally innocent," he wrote, "and their freedom to lead their own lives, depend upon the rulers' clear-headedness in the use of power. If their rulers are too weak, too scrupulous, too inexperienced, or too pure, their innocent pursuits of the good, however conceived, will sooner or later be disrupted."[16] This means that, when you are working your way through a gray area issue, you have to be able to answer this question: Do I have a plan that will actually work or will I fail the people who are depending on me and, at the same time, get my head handed to me?

Machiavelli wouldn't mind if you and others ignored his lessons, as long as you stayed in private life. But as soon as you take on responsibility for the lives and fortunes of others, you have to see and deal with the world as it is—a place in which all sorts of things happen: good and bad, evil and noble, inspiring and contemptible, planned and chaotic.

Practical Guidance: The Resilience Test

What does this worldview mean—in practical, on-the-ground terms—when you have to make hard, gray area decisions? What did it mean for Becky Friedman, who needed a way to handle Terry Fletcher and the pressure from her bosses? The basic answer is that, when you think about ways to resolve a gray area problem, you should ask yourself this question: How resilient is my plan and how resilient am I?

Five steps, all grounded in time-tested insights, can help you answer these questions. Each step is rooted in the long-standing tradition of eyes-open realism about the world and people around us, the perspective that Machiavelli articulated so brilliantly.

Map the Territory of Power and Interest

This guidance says you have to think hard about who wants what, how much they want it, and how powerful they are. Whether you like it or not, you are almost always surrounded by a force field of power and interest. You have to understand this force field and the options and risks it creates. This will help you anticipate the maneuvers of other parties, so you can respond to them more effectively. It will also help you devise a plan that will be resilient across these possibilities.

When you try to map the terrain of power and interest, be sure to think hard and realistically about your own self-interest. If you don't, the chances are that no one else will. Management isn't a job for martyrs. If you want to make contributions in the longer run, you have to survive the shorter run. If you aren't a player at the table, you can't influence the game. Machiavelli understood this clearly and put it bluntly. "A man with no position in society," he wrote, "cannot get a dog to bark at him."[17]

In Becky Friedman's situation, this analysis was straightforward. In personal terms, she liked her job and wanted to keep it. But her bosses didn't want Fletcher to get a bad evaluation, and they could make life miserable for her and her unit in a variety of ways. In the worst case, they could force her out of the company.

Jim Mullen was also surrounded by a force field of power and interest, but it was far more complicated. Consider, for example, just one element of it: the Food and Drug Administration. This agency would play an important role in whatever Mullen did about Tysabri, and it also regulated almost every aspect of Biogen Idec's business. In principle, the FDA was a neutral, independent, science-based arbiter of drug safety. In reality, it was also a player in a very complex, high-stakes financial and political contest. The FDA had vigorous, well-organized adversaries. Some critics believed it moved too slowly on promising new drugs. Others believed it was the captive of large pharmaceutical companies. At the time of the Tysabri controversy, the FDA was reeling from its recent approval and embarrassing withdrawal of Vioxx, a treatment for acute pain, that caused hundreds of deaths and serious cardiac problems, and the agency badly needed to restore its credibility.

In addition, Mullen knew that the FDA would soon be besieged by MS patients, their families, legislators, physicians, and others who wanted Tysabri to remain available, and these groups would be able to make powerful, heart-wrenching cases because MS sufferers urgently needed better treatments. Investors, competitors, key employees, and other groups also had strong interests in whatever Mullen did, so he would be making moves on a very complicated chessboard.

In situations like this, understanding power sometimes means looking accurately at the brute force—the "hard" power—that you and other parties can use. In Friedman's case, she believed that her bosses could fire her or force her out of the company. In Mullen's case, hard power consisted of the many ways a regulator like the FDA could make life miserable for a company.[18] In most cases, however, sophisticated parties rely heavily on "soft" power. They operate subtly and obliquely. Instead of threatening, they nudge and entice. They orchestrate feelings, pressures, and inducements. Sometimes, soft power involves revealing a sliver of the mailed fist inside the velvet glove, but its practitioners usually prefer to advance their interests in other ways.

These considerations matter from the very start of whatever process you create to deal with a gray area problem. Before you decide who will be part of a process, you have to understand what their agendas are and how much clout they have. So the first piece of practical guidance tells you to make a significant investment of time, thought, and imagination in thinking realistically, politically, and shrewdly about the power and interests of other parties. This will make you and your planning more resilient—by showing you whether you are operating in a minefield and indicating where some of the mines are buried.

Be Modest, Flexible, and Opportunistic

The second piece of guidance describes the most helpful mind-set for moving through complicated and hazardous political territory. Machiavelli is often interpreted as a cynic, but he wasn't. People who are always cynical are sometimes right, for the same reason that stopped clocks are right twice a day. But they miss opportunities because they are vigilantly paranoid and hunkered down, awaiting disaster. Stopped-clock optimists have a similar problem: sometimes they are exactly right and things turn out splendidly, but they can also stride confidently into walls or get their pockets picked.

Understanding what will work in the world as it is means thinking carefully, flexibly, and opportunistically. To be resilient, you have to adapt, maneuver, and persevere through whatever hazards and opportunities you encounter. Future events aren't the calculable vector sum of power and interest. Chance matters—sometimes greatly—as do complicated interactions that can be very hard to anticipate. So you have to be modest and even a little humble about how much you can understand and control. The wisdom behind the third question is an age-old view of life that the Renaissance essayist Michel de Montaigne summarized with an engraving on the necklace he wore. It said simply, "What do I know?"[19]

The managers dealing with Kathy Thompson had no idea what her real problem was. Jim Mullen didn't know whether the two cases of PML were a stunning coincidence or the tip of an awful iceberg. Becky Friedman knew her bosses wanted her to protect Terry Fletcher, but she had no idea how aggressively they would insist on this or how they might retaliate against her. These are hardly exceptional cases. In fact, they are simply instances of a fundamental characteristic of managerial work. C. Roland Christensen, a Harvard Business School professor who spent his career studying management, described the mandate for resiliency this way: "The uniqueness of a good general manager lies in the ability to lead effectively organizations whose complexity he or she can never fully understand, where the capacity to control directly the human and physical forces comprising the organization is severely limited, and where he or she must make or review and assume ultimate responsibility for present decisions which commit concretely major resources to a *fluid and unknown future*."[20]

Machiavelli and many other great thinkers would have endorsed this perspective. For example, Machiavelli compared fortune to a river.[21] Life and work bring long stretches of relative calm, unpredictably interspersed with periods of frightening, dangerous turbulence. Twenty years ago, no one expected the internet to radically transform life and work and to create extraordinary opportunities for entrepreneurs of all kinds. Ten years ago, few people expected a financial crisis to bring the world economy to the brink of another Great Depression.

Becky Friedman's resolution of her problem with Terry Fletcher is a clear example of how people and events can take unexpected twists. Friedman decided to try a counseling session with Fletcher. She told him she had definitely decided to give him a 2.5. He immediately objected and said that wasn't fair. Then she added that she wasn't going to put him on a PIP because she thought that would be demeaning. She also suggested he think hard about the recent hires in her department. They all had strong technical skills, and she added that he was unlikely to be happy or successful, surrounded by people with these backgrounds. She then suggested that Fletcher spend the next several months doing his job and looking carefully for another job.

Friedman was surprised and relieved when Fletcher smiled a little, relaxed, and said he would think about her suggestions. Apparently, he had already been toying with this idea. Fletcher spent the next several weeks looking for other positions, inside the company and elsewhere. Before too long, he found a good job with another firm.

It is easy to dismiss all this as just good luck. And Friedman did have some luck or, as Machiavelli and many other classical writers would see it, fate and fortune had smiled upon her. A dyed-in-the wool cynic might not have even attempted Friedman's approach, thinking the only options were doing what the bosses wanted or losing her job. A naive optimist might have ignored the threats from her bosses, skipped the counseling session, and given Fletcher a 2.5. Fortunately, Friedman was a pragmatist, prepared for a range of contingencies and flexible enough to take advantage of what actually did occur. She had no way of knowing whether the option of counseling Fletcher would work, but he smiled when she suggested looking for another job. Friedman was watching carefully, she saw his reaction, seized the opportunity, and took advantage of it.

Keep the Process Fluid and Flexible

Mapping the force field of power and relying on a flexible, opportunistic mind-set are important for dealing with gray area problems, but process also matters a lot, sometimes critically. Process always means deciding who will work with you on a problem and how everyone will work. But the third question can keep you from making these decisions naively. It tells you not to view process simply as a methodical, step-by-step way of working with other people to get information and analyze it. You need a process that is flexible, one that can adapt and change depending on the nasty surprises you encounter, the unexpected opportunities that pop up, and any political mines that go off. The first step in Becky Friedman's process for dealing with Terry Fletcher is an everyday example of this approach. She started with a low-key, under-the-radar counseling session with him. If it worked, as it did, she would have dodged a bullet. If it didn't, Friedman could try other options.

In the days after getting the PML news, Jim Mullen took a similar approach to what was, of course, a vastly more complex, uncertain, and politically charged problem than Friedman's. He immediately informed the FDA, overseas regulators, and the Biogen Idec board about the PML cases. Then he and his senior team spent a week scouring the world for information on PML to learn all they could about the risks to patients. Mullen didn't know whether a week of intensive effort would find evidence of a link between the new drug and a very rare disease but, like Friedman, Mullen decided to learn what he could without overcommitting.

Once he did know more—or found that he would be unable to learn more quickly—he could pursue other options. But this approach avoided the risk of a premature announcement that might undermine confidence in the drug, possibly trigger a panic among patients, and harm the company. It also gave Mullen and his senior team some time to carefully assess various possibilities and the steps Biogen could take if any of these possibilities became real.

In the end, Jim Mullen had started a process that lasted more than a year. After his week of information gathering, Mullen and his senior team decided to temporarily suspend distribution of Tysabri, rather than withdraw it permanently. This gave them the option to reintroduce the drug, depending on what more they learned and the protective measures they might be able to create. A suspension may have also placated, to a degree, the MS patients, physicians, and members of the US Congress who wanted Tysabri available.

Once he created some breathing room, Mullen initiated a long and complex process, aimed at making Tysabri available again. It involved MS and PML experts from around the world, drug regulators from several countries, careful scrutiny of the medical records of everyone who had taken Tysabri, and extensive outreach to doctors who treated MS and their patients. In the end, Biogen was able to develop protocols for determining which patients might be at risk for PML and for helping their doctors monitor them very carefully.

The outcome of this process wasn't ideal, which is often the case with gray area problems. By late 2014, more than 100,000 patients had taken Tysabri, but approximately 500 had contracted PML, more than 100 had died from it, and many others had various degrees of disability.[22] At the same time, however, hundreds of thousands of MS patients gained some relief from their illness. But no one could have anticipated this outcome in the weeks after the first two PML cases were discovered. A fluid, flexible, carefully managed process was crucial to finding a practical, acceptable, medically sound way of threading a very fine needle.

Be Ready to Play Hardball

Sometimes managers confront what Machiavelli called "necessity."[23] These are circumstances that give you no choice—if you want to resolve a hard problem, do it responsibly and avoid martyrdom. Resilience, in these circumstances, means pushing forward, despite clear obstacles, and sometimes it means playing hardball. This involves asserting your authority and using your power in ways that may feel uncomfortable, too aggressive, or ethically distressing.

If Aaron Feuerstein had permanently laid off some workers and closed parts of his operations, in order to preserve the jobs of others in the longer run, he would have seriously harmed the laid-off workers, who had few other options. Feuerstein would also have felt he was breaking his long-standing personal and family commitment to his workers. But Feuerstein didn't take these hard steps. Instead, he kept his hands clean, and the results were disastrous.

Becky Friedman took a different approach and played hardball with Terry Fletcher. At the beginning of their meeting, she told him that she had definitely decided to give him a 2.5. She also reminded him, unambiguously, of her power when she told him that she had decided not to give him a PIP. Friedman left no doubt she was the boss. She didn't waver when Fletcher protested, and she sent the clear message that she had the authority to make decisions about his future, despite Fletcher's relationship with the company executives.

But there was more to Friedman's tactics. She understood that hardball doesn't have to be a bludgeon and can take gentler, subtler forms. Notice that she moved back and forth between an "I am your boss" mode and an "I want to help you" mode. Friedman made it clear, for example, that she could put Fletcher on a PIP, but offered to save him from the embarrassment this would cause. Then she asked him to look around the organization and make his own judgments about his likelihood of succeeding. Fletcher remained unambiguously in charge. She was also clear about what she wanted to accomplish, which was moving Fletcher on, and what she wanted to avoid, which was trouble from her bosses, so she alternated gestures of friendship, support, and advice with clear reminders of her hard power.

Perceptions matter critically, regardless of how you play hardball. If you want to be effective in the world as it is, you have to think carefully about what others think. Perceptions matter in the moment, as they did in Friedman's meeting with Fletcher. They also matter afterwards, when people report on whatever you say and do. As these reports circulate, they strengthen or weaken your credibility, authority, and power. Of course, in an ideal world and in the best of organizations, substance dominates perception. But in the world as it often is, optics carry the day. The crucial question isn't what you say but what others hear, think, feel, remember, and act on.

Playing hardball and managing perceptions can leave you feeling uncomfortable—and it should. Most people don't want to work in organizations that operate this way. There are times, however, when meeting your responsibilities to others, in the world as it is, means getting your hands dirty. Machiavelli believed it was better for leaders to be honest, open, and virtuous. But he added that, if they want to survive, be effective, and meet their responsibilities, they sometimes had to do what was necessary. If they were squeamish, their lofty intentions would be little more than greeting card sentimentality, and the world would spin on unchanged.

Don't Excuse Yourself

The final piece of guidance is the briefest but basically the most important for managers. It is easy to misinterpret the third question and see it as advice to play it safe, take shortcuts, and look for the nearest exit when things get tough. This, however, profoundly misinterprets the realistic, pragmatic perspective.

One of Machiavelli's famous statements is that fortune favors the bold, and *The Prince*, his masterwork, can be read as an ode to the entrepreneurs of his era.[24] Some were business entrepreneurs: the Medici in Florence were inventing elements of modern, international banking, but the true entrepreneurs of the Renaissance were rethinking, reshaping, and disrupting long-established institutions and practices.[25] The entrepreneurs of the Renaissance were responsible, in large part, for many of our contemporary ideas about art, politics, community, politics, government, personal identity, and religion.

Realism isn't fatalism. It doesn't say you can't do much and should stay safely on the sidelines. It says, instead, that you have to ask what will work—if you think and act with persistence, dedication, creativity, a willingness to take prudent risks, cleverness, and politically astute timing. Neither Becky Friedman nor Jim Mullen had any guarantee that their efforts, one lasting several weeks and the other several years, would work. But, if they hadn't moved ahead thoughtfully and astutely, they never would have succeeded, and the world would have been a lesser place.

Practical, Everyday Tools

We have now examined three of the great humanist questions—one focused on consequences, another on duties, and this last one on cold, hard pragmatics. Each question has stood the test of time. Each has clear, practical implications for grappling with gray area problems. So how much progress have we have now made? Do these three questions give us the tools we need for resolving gray area problems? The answer is that we have made a good start, but only if we use the questions in the right way and recognize what they can and cannot do.

The three questions are tools for triggering, sharpening, and improving your judgment. But they aren't the kind of tools you find in a high-tech laboratory. Those are sophisticated, precision instruments, designed for specialists working in carefully controlled conditions. In contrast, the five questions resemble everyday tools. They are basic and versatile, and need to be used in certain ways.

First, these tools work best if you use them together. Doing this will give you a much better grasp of complexity of gray area problems. Becky Friedman, for example, had to consider consequences: How would keeping Fletcher affect the performance of her team? She also had to consider duties: Could she find ways to treat him with respect and dignity? And she had to be pragmatic: How would she deal with the unsubtle pressures from her bosses? Friedman clearly needed all three tools to really understand the challenge she faced.

Using the three tools together can also help you narrow your options and focus your analysis. This is another way in which the questions can work like a funnel. The first question can lead you to drop some options because their costs and risks outweigh their benefits. When you ask the second question, you may reject some other options because they violate your basic duties. And the third question can lead you to reject other options because you simply can't see them working.

What happens if you don't use the three tools together? The risk is that you will miss something really important. Each tool, used exclusively, can be inadequate, misleading, or even hazardous—the equivalent of trying to use a hammer for every household problem. If you focus only on consequences, you can overlook your basic duties to others. Focusing solely on duties can mean neglecting larger, broader consequences. And, if you focus solely on what will work, you can cross the ill-defined line that separates skepticism, pragmatism, and realism from shady or corrupt behavior. In short, a very important reason to use the three questions together is that they balance, offset, and correct each other.

But, despite these advantages, the three tools aren't enough. Sometimes they point you in conflicting directions when you are looking for a way out of a gray area. Consequences and duties can clash with each other, and both can conflict with pragmatic considerations. Also, there can be conflicts within each perspective. Should Jim Mullen and Biogen, for example, have focused more heavily on the lives and rights of patients with MS or the rights and lives of patients at risk for PML?

The interim verdict on the first three questions is that they are important and useful. They can dispel a good deal of gray, but not enough. To finally resolve gray area problems, you have to ask and answer two other fundamental questions.

5

Who Are We?

In 1956, William Whyte published *The Organization Man*. This was one of the last century's most important studies of business, and its ideas still shape—and distort—much of what we still think about organizations. The book was a harsh account of what happened to the human beings, mostly men, who spent their lives working in the large companies that dominated the American economy. They became, Whyte argued, tiny cogs in giant machines. As a result, their lives were squeezed down, hollowed out, and impoverished.[1]

Whyte's book is a compelling account of the hazards of organizational life, but only a partial picture. The reality is that we are surrounded, almost all the time, by organizations. We begin life in families, perhaps the oldest organization of

95

all. We work, play, worship, and shop in organizations. Hence, we are all, inescapably and pervasively, "organization men."

This reality is captured in an old African adage. It says, "I am because we are." This statement has a broad sweep. It encompasses Whyte's point that organizations and communities do things *to* us—they limit, impair, and restrict us. The saying also reminds us of the many things that organizations and communities do *for* us—providing basic needs, meeting wants and desires, and opening up opportunities. But the adage says even more. It captures an elemental feature of the human condition, one with direct relevance to managers facing gray area decisions.[2] It tells us that organizations and communities define who we are and shape what we do in profound and decisive ways.

The fourth humanist question asks managers facing difficult decisions to see themselves as creatures whose identities are woven into the fabric of their surrounding communities. It then encourages them to seek options that will reflect, express, and give reality to the norms and values of the communities to which they belong.

The Mystic Chords of Memory

To understand what the fourth question is asking us, we need to shift our mind-sets. Each of the previous humanist questions assumes a world of autonomous individuals. From this perspective, each of us is an independent agent, a self-contained unit, a separate monad. The first three questions all made this assumption: what individuals do has consequences, each of us has duties, and we all pursue our own self-interest, banging against each other like billiard balls. And this is, of course, a perfectly natural way to think. All of us know our own minds, we have the direct experience of making decisions, and we act as autonomous physical creatures.

In contrast, the fourth question puts individuality and autonomy to the side. It says we are deeply social creatures. Our relationships immerse us in webs of expectations, commitments, routine practices, taboos, and aspirations. Put succinctly, it is relationships, values, and norms that make us who we are. That is, of course, a broad and abstract statement. To see what it means in concrete terms, we will turn to a vivid, dramatic situation. It is a variant of a classic dilemma, popularized by William Godwin, a seventeenth-century novelist, journalist, and political philosopher, probably best known as the father of Mary Shelley, the author of *Frankenstein*.[3]

Suppose you are walking down a street, relaxing and enjoying the fine weather. But you smell something odd and, when you turn a corner, you see a building on fire. In the next moment, you see three children inside the building. You believe you can save them, without risking your life, and you start running into the building. But then you notice another child in the building, standing alone, and this child is yours. The fire is raging, and you can go into the building just once before it collapses. What do you do? Do you save the three children or save your child?

The three questions in the previous chapters all seem to suggest the same answer. In terms of consequences, three lives outweigh one. In terms of duties, all the children have an equal right to live, so you may have a stronger duty to save the three. In terms of what will work in the world as it is, both options—saving three children or saving your child—seem feasible. So the three first three questions seem to say you should save the three children and let your child perish. But something seems wrong with this logic.

For one thing, it can spiral into paralyzing philosophical disputation, with rationality endlessly chasing its own tail. Maybe, in the long run, the net, net consequences for everyone are best served if people put their own families first. Maybe there is an argument that our duties to family members supersede duties to others. Maybe you have no duty to save any children, so you are free to save your child. In all likelihood, other arguments could be laboriously constructed in order to justify doing what most parents would want to do, instinctively and urgently: run into the building and save their own child. The analytical twists and turns seem like unnecessary and hyperrational efforts to justify a simple truth that parents know and feel.

In fact, there seems to be something wrong with individuals who need elaborate reasons to take care of people close to them. The men and women who support their families, remain faithful to their partners, and sacrifice for the people in their lives don't typically do these things because it is their duty or because this behavior maximizes the net, net consequences for society. These highly analytical, rational approaches to problems can reduce human beings to stick figures. Our true humanity is not what we are, stripped of our important relationships and viewed as thinking machines tallying consequences or prioritizing duties. For most people, taking care of one's children isn't just something parents do. It is a large part of who they are.

Why do relationships matter so much? The answer is partly that relationships create norms and values that guide our decisions. But relationships do much more. They shape us. They define our identities. They give meaning, purpose, and structure to our lives. They are constitutive: they make us who we are.[4] In other words, we are deeply, intrinsically, and inescapably relational beings.

Constitutive relationships have roots in a shared past, in what Abraham Lincoln called "the mystic chords of memory."[5] They also involve shared aspirations for the future, a sense that everyone in a group or community is bound together on a common journey.[6] Constitutive relationships cannot be reduced to precise analytical terms, but that doesn't make these obligations less important or less compelling. It simply puts them in the category of truths that Blaise Pascal described when he wrote, "The heart has its reasons that reason does not know."[7]

An earlier chapter criticized Aaron Feuerstein for his decisions after the disaster at Malden Mills, but many people found something deeply admirable about him. After the fire, a nationally televised interview showed Feuerstein and the head of the Malden Mills union teasing each other in a good-natured way. The two men clearly respected and liked each other. Interviews with several employees revealed the same thing. In fact, Feuerstein's nickname was "the mensch of Malden Mills." The Yiddish word refers to someone of high integrity or, in everyday terms, "a stand-up guy." For Feuerstein, like his father before him, Malden Mills, its workers, and their communities were inextricably bound up with his daily work, his life, his ideals, and his sense of who he was. His relationships defined him.

The Network of Mutuality

If managers ignore their constitutive relationships when they face hard decisions, they are not only rejecting parts of themselves. They are also rejecting a long-standing perspective on our common human experience. Over the centuries, the idea that human nature is profoundly social has taken many different forms. The sacred Hindu text, the Upanishads, explains this perspective with a simple metaphor. It says, "As all the spokes are fastened to the hub and the rim of a wheel, so to one's self are fastened all beings, all the gods, all the worlds, all the breaths, and all these bodies."[8] In the West, Aristotle's succinct and famous statement of this perspective was his definition of human beings as political or social animals.[9]

During the Middle Ages, the Western tradition transformed this idea into a worldview called "the great chain of being." It said the universe was organized like a vast corporate organization chart. God presided over ranks of angels. Below them, on earth, were kings, then other royalty, then other strata of society. Further down, in the underworld, there was Satan who presided over the ranks of fallen angels. This way of thinking—the view that all life or all humanity and perhaps all of reality is deeply one—began to recede during the Renaissance and, for many people, the emergence of modern science made it to a charming metaphor rather than a description of reality.

And yet the idea of some vast, encompassing "we" remains powerful, and we often hear variations on this theme. Martin Luther King Jr., for example, composed a beautiful, lyrical version of the idea. In his *Letter from Birmingham Jail*, King wrote, "We are caught in an inescapable network of mutuality, tied in a single garment of destiny."[10] Most religions today accept some version of the idea King expressed, and so do atheists.[11] Albert Einstein, for example, wrote, "It seems to me that the idea of a personal God is an anthropological concept which I cannot take seriously . . . Science has been charged with undermining morality, but the charge is unjust. A man's ethical behavior should be based effectually on sympathy, education, and social ties and needs; no religious basis is necessary."[12]

In fact, a scientific perspective can reinforce the idea of deep human bonds. Evolutionary theory treats human beings as just another of the species that originated when a lightning bolt or a lava flow heated a pool of carbon-based muck and somehow produced molecules that replicated, survived, and evolved. Yet even from this perspective, the notion of deep psychological and emotional bonds—largely unconscious, pervasive and powerful—remains plausible.

We have already noted that our ancient ancestors were the creatures that were more sensitive to relationships and more inclined to collaborate and hence had a better chance of surviving and passing along their genes.[13] But evidence of many kinds suggests we are profoundly social beings. For example, anthropologists and others have studied the occasional reports of so-called feral children—who were raised by bears or other animals and, for years, had no human contact. Once they were found, these children had serious difficulty learning language and showed little interest in other people; some even had trouble learning to walk upright.[14] These reports, as well as psychological studies of abandoned children raised in abusive institutional settings, point to the same conclusion as evolutionary science: from our earliest years and at the level of basic brain structure and development, we are relational beings.

In short, a wide range of long-standing scientific, philosophical, and religious perspectives all point us to the same conclusion. When we make hard decisions, we need to pay close and sensitive attention to our defining relationships and to the values and norms they create and support. Our decisions should recognize, in the words of sociologist Philip Selznick, that "in the beginning is society, not the individual."[15] This means looking closely at the norms and values of the organizations and communities around us and trying to discern what they mean for gray area problems.

But how? To answer this question, we will look closely at a hard gray area problem that confronted the CEO of a major company. This incident shows the practical challenges of answering the fourth question, and it will also help illustrate important practical guidelines for meeting these challenges.

The Practical Challenges

In November 2007, a photographer snapped a painful photograph of Jerry Yang, the CEO and cofounder of Yahoo!. Yang was testifying before a US congressional committee about his company's role in the arrest of Shi Tao, a Chinese journalist and dissident. In Western eyes, Shi Tao's offense was inconsequential; but, after a quick, secret trial, he was sentenced to ten years in prison. The photograph captured the moment when Yang turned around and faced Shi Tao's parents, who were sitting in the spectators' gallery immediately behind him. Yang's face seemed to be filled with sorrow, remorse, and shame.

His reaction may well have reflected a sense that he and his company had violated values and ignored relationships that were central to his life and to Yahoo!'s identity. Yang, his family, and the company he helped create had eagerly embraced and benefited from the American ethos of freedom, opportunity, and individual liberty. Yang's parents were Chinese, and his mother had brought him to the United States when he was ten years old. When he arrived, the only English word he knew was "shoe." He later reflected, "We got made fun of a lot at first. I didn't even know who the faces were on the paper money." Within three years, however, Yang was fluent in English. He excelled in high school and was working on his doctorate at Stanford University when he and Jerry Filo created a simple internet list of their favorite websites and circulated it to their friends. Within a few years, this part-time project had evolved into Yahoo!, a multibillion-dollar company. Now, because of the Shi Tao situation, Yang and his company were being excoriated—by customers, human rights organizations, the media, and members of Congress.

The Shi Tao incident originated in the early 2000s. Like many other Western companies, Yahoo! had begun building major operations in China. As a condition of doing business there, these companies agreed to follow China's laws and regulations restricting freedom of speech. Then, in 2005, Shi Tao used his Yahoo! e-mail account to send a document to Western reporters that described Chinese government restrictions on media coverage of the anniversary of the Tiananmen Square protests. This document had been widely circulated among Chinese media organizations and was hardly a high-level state secret. Police officers representing Chinese state security went to a Yahoo! office, met with the office manager, and presented official documents requesting the name associated with the e-mail account. The office manager provided Shi Tao's name. He was arrested immediately and, within months, sentenced to prison.

What does the Yahoo! situation tell us about the practical challenges of using the fourth question—Who are we?—for resolving gray area problems? Basically, it reveals three serious issues. The first is that managers and their companies have many relationships and hence are committed to a wide range of values and norms. So how do they decide which relationships and which norms and values matter most in a particular situation? Should you focus primarily on the values and norms of your team, your entire organization, your local communities, or, in the Yahoo! case, your home country? And what about the norms and values that really matter in your personal or family life or, if you are religious, in your faith community?

The second problem is deciding what to do when some of your values and norms seem to contradict others. For example, at the time of the Shi Tao incident, Yahoo! was committed to "open access to information and communication on a global basis." The company was also committed to "providing individuals with easy access to information and opportunities to openly communicate and exchange views and opinions." Another of its values was recognizing that "each country enacts its own laws in accordance with its own local norms and mores, and we must comply with applicable laws."[16] Most companies around the world have a similar range of fundamental commitments, beliefs, and values. Some are stated, some are implicit. All are typically important but, quite often, particularly in gray area cases, some of these values and commitments contradict others.

The third practical challenge is that basic values, like those in Yahoo!'s statement of its beliefs, are typically expressed in vague, abstract terms. What, for example, do integrity or quality really mean? As a result, managers have to fill in the expansive blanks and decide what these broad, aspirational terms actually mean in particular situations. And, when managers try to do this, they have no exemption from biased thinking. You shouldn't assume, even if you have spent years working in an organization, that you know with certainty what its defining commitments mean in a particular situation. Aaron Feuerstein seems to have made that mistake, with his sweeping, initial, instinctive decision to rebuild everything. The title "manager" and its accompanying authority provide no exemption from distorted thinking.

Even worse, working with others often doesn't necessarily solve this problem, and the reason is groupthink. The organizational version of this problem, which we can observe almost every day, is relatively benign. We see the full danger of groupthink in the many vast, horrendous, social crimes that are the perverted achievements of people whose defining relationships are suffused with the wrong values and norms. The Nazis, for example, may have enacted what were widely shared, yet heinous values.[17] Montaigne's observation—"I know of no greater miracle or monster than myself"—also applies to organizations and communities.[18] It seems likely that we humans have a factory-installed instinct to be vigilant and suspicious about outsiders and to prefer our fellow insiders, and we sometimes do this blindly, passionately, and immorally.[19]

In short, the fourth crucial question creates serious challenges when we try to use it to resolve a gray area problem. Relationships, values and norms are powerful forces. They shape, define, and express some of our highest aspirations. We should not and perhaps cannot ignore them. But when we try to answer the fourth question, we have to somehow decide which norms and values matter most. We have to figure out which ones go to the head of the line when conflicts occur. And we have to find ways to see, clearly and objectively, what our most important norms and values tell us to do in particular situations.

Practical Guidance

Fortunately, there are four steps you can take—each reflecting important, long-standing ideas—to meet these challenges head-on and put the fourth question to good use.

Don't Start Here

The first guideline is simple—and surprising. It says that you should think twice before you follow a standard piece of advice. Managers often hear that, when they face hard problems, they should put the norms and values of their organizations and communities front and center. But this approach is risky, and the reason is the murkiness and ambiguity of these norms and values.

To reduce this risk, it is useful to start thinking through a gray area situation by first focusing on the three questions discussed in the previous chapters. They have stood the test of time because they are, among other things, strong antidotes to subjective bias. The first question says to look at the full range of possible consequences. This means working hard, with other people, to think broadly, honestly, and objectively about all the important elements of a situation. The second question focuses on duties. This means asking: What duties do I have to other people because they are my fellow human beings, because of the law or because of commitments my organization has made? The highly pragmatic third question pushes you to look as realistically as you can at the risks, uncertainties, and politics of situations.

These first three questions ask you to look externally, objectively, systematically, and factually. Will this wring out all the bias? No. But nothing can do that. Whatever decisions we make are—inevitably—as Nietzsche put it, "human, all too human."[20] But starting with the first three questions is a way to create the best possible foundation of reliable facts and sound judgments for whatever decisions you have to make. Once you have this foundation in place, you can step back from the problem and think about it in terms of relationships, values, and norms.

Shut Down the Analytical Machinery

For managers facing hard problems, answering the question Who are we? requires a different kind of thinking. Managers typically want to analyze the issue, figure out what to do, and get started doing it. But answering the fourth question means looking away from the intricacies and nuances of a problem and trying instead to see its full context. This means dimming the sharp, bright light of analysis and trying to get a fresh perspective.

Chester Barnard, one of the great organizational theorists of the twentieth century, was a penetrating thinker who spent the early decades of his career running companies. He believed that understanding the larger human and organizational context of problems was a crucial skill of successful executives. He called this skill "the art of sensing the whole."[21] This was a partly conscious, partly intuitive sense of how an organization really worked and what really mattered in the organization. It was a feel, in part, for all informal, subtle, psychological, and emotional relationships among its members.

Sharply focused analytical effort can make it much harder to develop a "sense of the whole." Consider the example of Sherlock Holmes. He is known for his steel-trap deductive analysis. But Holmes did more than simply observe and analyze. His creator, Arthur Conan Doyle, sometimes described him slouching in an armchair in his small sitting room, smoking a pipe and staring aimlessly into space. In these moments, Holmes was musing on a problem, turning it over in his mind, and looking for new angles.[22] Holmes was doing a version of design thinking.[23] This is a way of working on problems that many organizations have recently adopted. It is open, flexible, relaxed, looks from different angles, toys with possibilities, and avoids rushing to judgment. Design thinking is qualitative rather than quantitative, zigzag rather than linear. It involves alertness to underlying themes and emerging patterns. It avoids quickly intuited or carefully calculated "right" answers and depends instead on looser, ruminative approaches. This kind of thinking draws on our full humanity—on instinct, feeling, intuition, and sensibility, rather than raw brainpower and acute analytical focus.

In a talk several years ago at Harvard Business School, Warren Buffett told students that they should find some way to "give away" any IQ points they had above 130.[24] Buffett was clearly suggesting that analytical intelligence is valuable but can also be a trap. To answer the subtle question of Who are we?, you need to stop hammering on the anvil of a problem and take time to reflect on its context. The next three guidelines offer ways to do this. Each suggests a different focus for this reflection: your real self-interest, your organization's story, and others' likely perspective on the problem you are dealing with.

Reflect on Your Real Self-Interest

Underlying the fourth humanist question and all the practical guidance in this chapter is a radical idea: that we may not really understand our own self-interest, if we think of ourselves simply as autonomous actors. Of course, this is a natural way to think and, from Machiavelli's perspective, it makes particular sense. As he sees it, we live and work in an uncertain, competitive, and political world. When we are with family and friends, we can think differently but, when we leave home, we have to watch our backs and take care of ourselves.

But notice a feature of this way of thinking. It is basically black and white. It draws sharp lines: between personal life and work life, between selfishness and altruism, between what you get and what others get. This binary world is deeply at odds with the perspective of the fourth question. A clear implication of the African aphorism is that, by pursuing the interests of others, we pursue our own interests, because all these interests are so tightly meshed. And this isn't because we are continuously contracting with each other and making a long series of deals that serve our interests. It is because our human fates are joined in profound ways.

Think, for example, about members of families or members of military units that have seen combat. In these cases, "we" is much more than a collection of individuals. Each individual's identity is defined, in part, by membership in the group. Hence, what is best for each individual is, in part, what is best for everyone. In many cases, family members and soldiers can't answer the question, What should I do? unless they also answer the question, What should we do?

This perspective suggests that managers faced with hard decisions should be careful not to view their situation solely in simplistic terms that assumes their gain is another's loss and vice versa. Aaron Feuerstein had a personal commitment to his workers and their communities; he wasn't calculating when and what he would gain from them. And hardly anyone would want Jim Mullen at Biogen, or anyone else in a comparable position of trust and power, to be calculating personal gain or organizational gain at the expense of the lives and health of others. Our society depends critically on leaders who understand that we all share common interests—in civility, trust, openness, and a commitment to social good—and all benefit from common endeavors to support these aims and interests, even though none of us can calculate our personal sliver of gain from these social investments.

Classical Chinese philosophy emphasizes *yin* and *yang*. It suggests that, at the deeper levels of individual and social complexity, important realities are interdependent, commingled, joint, and connected. In other words, what matters for each of us is what matters for all of us. This suggests that managers faced with hard problems need to step back and spend some time asking what higher, broader purposes are at stake in their decision. This may not, in the end, be the decisive factor in a decision, but it can reveal facets of a situation that are long-term, subtle, and important. These facets can easily be overlooked by managers trained to process every problem through the standard analytical techniques, and a good way to reduce this risk is by relying on an age-old way of understanding reality: by thinking in terms of stories, rather than data and analysis.

Reflect on Your Organization's Story

Most organizations today have credos and mission statements. Unfortunately, these are often lifeless documents, decorating walls or embalmed under glass. Nevertheless, for a manager facing a hard problem, a mission statement or credo is usually worth a look. It can serve as a reminder of the larger aims to which the organization has committed itself. And in some cases, credos and mission statements can be particularly valuable—if they have been created recently or tested recently and reflect serious attention and real commitment. But it is also important to look more broadly and, in particular, to understand the stories that reveal the norms, values, and relationships that define your organization.

For millennia, humanity has relied on stories as the most powerful way to understand and express who "we" are. And almost everyone still enjoys stories today. But do stories matter in organizations? We no longer forage and hunt and live around campfires or huddled in caves. Maybe stories are just relics: charming, old-fashioned, and roundabout ways of conveying what should be stated clearly and succinctly. We work in modern, fast-paced, technology-driven organizations. Instead of telling a story, why not just get to the point?

There are several answers to this question, and they all help explain the practical value of the fourth enduring question. One answer is that stories convey truths more powerfully than propositions. They stick in ways that bullet points don't and can't. Stories engage, not just our minds, but our hearts and spirits. They can resonate with our personal experiences, which makes their underlying messages vivid and real. Stories also give us a sense of getting down to the basics—which is the idea behind the classic view, sometimes attributed to Aristotle, that history tells us what happened and literature tells us what happens.[25]

The idea that stories communicate in distinctive, powerful ways is another example of striking convergence between contemporary social science and ancient wisdom and insights. Jerome Bruner, one of the most important cognitive psychologists of the twentieth century, has long argued that our minds have evolved to frame and grasp reality in two different ways. One is propositional and depends on clarity, logic, and formal structure. The other is narrative—in other words, story-based. Bruner, along with scholars in a wide range of fields, such as law, anthropology, and cognitive science, believes that much of what we view as objective reality consists of narratives or stories that are widely accepted within groups or entire cultures.[26]

Adrienne Rich, a contemporary poet, wrote, "The story of our lives becomes our lives."[27] This observation applies to organizations as well. In many organizations today, the real values and norms are expressed in stories. Sometimes they describe what the founders did, how they thought, what they sacrificed, and what they fought for. Other stories describe difficult moments, crises, or critical decisions in which an organization's leaders, past or present, had to make choices that revealed what they most cared about. Above all, these stories say what the organization is really committed to and the larger purpose it aims to serve. In short, the answer to the fourth humanist question—Who are we?—often consists of stories that describe what "we" have done in critical moments and why "we" did it. These are typically stories of commitment, struggle, and purpose.

This remains true today. Human nature hasn't changed during the recent centuries of stunning technological advances. We remain the creatures we have always been. This is why every organization has stories—even small organizations, like departments and work teams, and new organizations, like entrepreneurial ventures. It is also why it is valuable, for highly practical reasons, to understand what these stories are when you face a gray area problem.

Recall Becky Friedman's situation. She faced the tricky problem of dealing with an employee who had strong support from her bosses but was failing to do his job. Friedman was new to her company. The company, an entrepreneurial venture, was only a few years old, and the "organization" in which she worked was the team of fourteen people she headed. Nevertheless, there were two narratives that helped Friedman understand the full dimensions of the situation she faced.

One story described her long slog as a woman in computer science. Friedman had always been an outsider. Even though she was a talented programmer, she also understood, from her undergraduate education and her work experience, what it was like to be marginalized socially—which was Terry Fletcher's situation on her team. He wasn't making the grade, he knew it, and he knew that almost everyone else knew it. At the same time, Friedman had another story in mind. It described what the rest of her team, aside from Fletcher, understood and really cared about: exceptional professional performance. Her team consistently overachieved on the company's performance metrics, as a result of talent and long hours of work. She felt proud of this accomplishment, and so did the members of her team. Their story described their week-by-week and month-by-month efforts, working hard and smart, to achieve well-earned organizational stardom.

Friedman understood the larger context of the Terry Fletcher situation, and this helped her handle it effectively.

As we saw in the last chapter, Friedman did an excellent job of answering the third question—What will work in the world as it is?—and maneuvered astutely and opportunistically across a political minefield. But she was also successful because these two stories illuminated larger social realities: the ethos of the winning team and the frustration of feeling, as Terry Fletcher did, on the outside looking in. This enabled her to turn her meetings with Fletcher into useful and sympathetic counseling sessions that eased his way out of the company and ultimately into a better job.

In short, you can use your own sense of the key experiences and stories of your organization to answer the fourth question. Put differently, what matters to you may well shed light on what matters to others. Hence, when you face a hard gray area issue, you should spend a few minutes stepping back and trying to understand the situation in terms of some of the defining experiences in your organization's history that matter *to you* and help you understand what your organization stands for.

From this perspective, a manager facing a hard problem isn't simply trying to find the right answer. He or she is also writing a sentence or paragraph in the long narrative of an organization's history. By putting a particular problem in this larger context, a manager can sometimes see elements that would otherwise be overlooked, eliminate some options that pass the tests of consequences, duties, and pragmatism, and elicit more support for whatever he or she decides—because others will feel that the manager's decision is helping to strengthen, build, or protect the values and norms that define their organization.

Explain Yourself

Another way to get a clearer understanding of important norms and values is to try a simple exercise. It is also a way to avoid the risk of becoming the type of "organization man" that William Whyte warned about. In other words, this exercise can help managers facing a gray area problem resist the pressure to do something about the problem, do it right away, deal with its immediate financial, organizational, and political elements, and then move on to other work.

The exercise is this. Imagine you are standing in front of each of the groups that will be affected by your decision. Imagine you have just explained your decision to them. Then ask yourself: How will they react? What will they think and feel and say? What you would be thinking and feeling, if you were one of them? Will they see you as one of them, struggling to express and live by important, shared values and norms or will they see you as an outsider, an alien, as someone who doesn't "get it" and doesn't belong?

The aim of the exercise is getting a clearer understanding of the implicit norms, values, and ideals that really matter to the people your decision will affect—and doing this *before* you make a decision, so your understanding of these values can shape your actual decision. To see what this means in practice, try rethinking the Shi Tao incident.

Yahoo! faced a very difficult issue in China, once the state security officers appeared at the Yahoo! offices. But the company might have handled it better, if its executives had followed some version of this exercise in the months or years before Shi Tao's arrest and imprisonment. They could have asked themselves how they would handle a situation like the one that actually occurred—after all, a request from Chinese state security authorities for personal information about a political dissident was hardly an unlikely scenario. And if they ultimately decided to handle it in the way they actually did, Yahoo!'s executives might have understood how difficult it would be to explain this decision, in terms of basic values and commitments, to everyone it would affect.

Would this exercise have made a difference? There is no way to know. But it might have become clear that doing what Yahoo! actually did was an untenable response to the situation, and the company might have taken some useful precautions. For example, the office manager who identified the journalist had no guidelines or training for handling situations with state officials. There was no senior Yahoo! official available for him to consult. And the information the police wanted was readily available, not stored in a remote server or protected by passwords or approvals. In contrast, Google kept its personal identification data on servers in Hong Kong.

None of these steps would have eliminated the problem, but some combination of them might have given the company time to work on tactics and perhaps negotiate with the Chinese officials. Just as important, steps like these would have enabled Jerry Yang and Yahoo! to explain, to critics and to Shi Tao's parents, that they had done all they could, aside from leaving China altogether, to protect the privacy of Yahoo! customers and stand up for Western values of free speech. Yahoo! and its employees would also have known that the company had done all it could do to adhere to the values that defined the organization.

The practical guidance for answering the fourth question—working first on the other three questions, loosening your thinking and trying to get "a sense of the whole," reflecting on your real self-interest and your organization's defining stories, and testing how well you can explain possible decisions in terms of basic norms and values in a company—seems to add yet another layer of complexity to resolving gray area problems. But these steps don't *create* complexity. They reflect it and reveal it. The complexity is out there in the world. It is an intrinsic part of gray area problems. And, sooner or later, you have to grapple with the complexity when you face a gray area problem. Yahoo! learned this the hard way when it brushed up against the buzz saw of complexity, because it had failed to anticipate how doing business in China would challenge its important relationships, values, and norms.

Clarity and Simplicity

The fourth question is another basic tool for improving your judgment about gray area problems. If you use this question and the other three, you will understand the full human complexities of these problems. We all suffer and we all seek joy and happiness, so consequences really matter. We share the same humanity, so we owe each other basic duties. We are vulnerable to chance, surprises, and malevolence, which is why pragmatic, realistic thinking is so important. And we are all shaped and defined by communities around us, their "mystic chords of memory" and their sense of shared purpose.

Your answers to these questions are critically important for resolving gray area problems, but they aren't enough. If you have serious responsibilities, at work or elsewhere in life, you have to do more than grasp complexities. Responsibility also means deciding and acting. At some point, you have to say to others and to yourself: "This is what we are going to do and this is how we will do it." In the end, what matters for resolving a gray area problem isn't complexity. It is clarity and simplicity.

But what is simplicity in a gray area and how do you find it? A powerful answer to this question comes from Oliver Wendell Holmes Jr. He is best known as an associate justice of the US Supreme Court, and his opinions shaped much of American life. Holmes's thinking about complexity was influenced by a deep humanist perspective. As a judge, for example, he moved away from legal formalism, with its sharp focus on the precise meaning and application of laws, toward legal realism—which he summarized in the sentence "The life of the law has not been logic; it has been experience."[28]

Even before his long legal career Holmes had grappled hard with complexity. He grew up in Boston, the son of an important doctor and scientist. Though he spent his early years living comfortably and attending Harvard College, he volunteered to fight in the Civil War. Holmes was seriously wounded on three different occasions and, each time, once he recovered, he returned to combat. During his early years, Holmes also struggled to comprehend how the country he was fighting to preserve could be dedicated to liberty and yet treat some human beings as private property.

Holmes the jurist and military hero was also Holmes the serious moralist. He searched hard for truth, but understood how hard it was to find, in the law and in life. And he put this plainly in a letter to a longtime friend and described the kind of simplicity that, for him, mattered most. "The only simplicity for which I would give a straw," Holmes wrote, "is that which is on the other side of the complex."[29]

In other words, there are two kinds of simplicity. One overlooks, ignores, or dismisses complexity. It's the kind of simplicity you see when somebody looks briefly at a really difficult problem and then announces, with certainty, the precise right answer. Holmes thought this kind of simplicity was worthless. He only cared about simplicity that has been shaped, tested, and forged by the full, real complexities of a problem or situation.

But where does this simplicity come from? If you are facing a hard gray area problem, how do you find it? The next chapter, which focuses on the fifth great humanist question, answers these two questions and explains how to finally resolve gray area problems.

6

What Can I Live With?

The fifth question gives us the final, critical step for resolving gray area problems—and it does this with a striking message. It says that, no matter how hard you work, no matter how good your analysis is, and no matter how carefully you think about consequences, duties, practicalities, and values, you often don't *find* an answer to a gray area problem. What do you do then? Basically, you *create* the answer, and you do this by making a decision you can live with—as a manager and as a human being. That is how you resolve a gray area issue.

What does it mean to "live with" a decision? Sometimes it means you have to accept or tolerate a decision. You did all you could, but you've only met a minimum standard of acceptability. Often, gray area problems don't have win-win options. Your job is making the least bad choice, and the "success" that you live with is success with complications, sometimes serious ones. In the case of Tysabri, the drug returned to the market and alleviated a great deal of suffering, but it also risked lives. In other cases, you work hard on your own and with others, and you find a creative, practical approach to a gray area problem. You live with it and feel proud about it. That is how Becky Friedman felt about her efforts with Terry Fletcher.

However, regardless of whether your decision meets a minimal or aspirational standard, you live with your decision on a gray area problem in a deeper way. You are accountable—to others and to yourself—for what you decide. As a manager, you will be held accountable—legally, organizationally, financially, and in other ways. But you will also have serious personal responsibility for whatever you decide, and that is the focus of the fifth question.

This responsibility runs deep. You resolve a gray area decision by saying explicitly: "This is what I have decided and this is what we are going to do." But that isn't all you are deciding. You are also deciding, inevitably, the answer to the first four enduring questions. Your decision says—based on your personal judgment—which consequences, duties, pragmatic factors, and values matter most and which matter less. And you can't escape this responsibility. Gray area decisions inevitably reflect and reveal the personal priorities of the person who makes them.

Because gray area decisions are yours in this personal way, the fifth question pushes you to reflect seriously on what *you* can live with. Gray area problems test competence and character. They are intersections of work and life. To answer them well, you have to think hard about what you really care about, as a manager and a person, and what these convictions mean for the decision you are making. Grappling with the fifth enduring question can take real courage. A retired senior executive, looking back at her long and successful career, reflected, "We really want someone or some rule to tell us what to do, but sometimes there isn't one and you have to decide what the most relevant rules or principles are in this particular case. You can't escape this responsibility."

Fortunately, the fifth question—What can I live with?—is old. For millennia, in both the East and the West, it has challenged many extraordinarily thoughtful and insightful men and women. And we can turn to them to understand, in depth, what the question is really asking and to get some practical guidance for answering it well. As with the previous questions, you will see that process matters. But the process that matters for answering the fifth question well is a process, not with other people, but within yourself. This process consists of some final steps you can take to reflect on a gray area problem before you commit to a decision.

Character and Judgment

In the end, a manager's character, convictions, and values matter critically for resolving gray area problems—for reasons that the wisest and most acute observers of the human condition have given, in various ways, over many centuries. Their answer says, in essence, that for really hard decisions, your judgment is the decisive factor, and judgment reflects character. In other words, like the DNA double helix, judgment and character are deeply intertwined.

For example, for Aristotle, the right answer to a difficult problem was the golden mean. In other words, the best decisions avoid excesses. Too much courage becomes recklessness, too much prudence becomes cowardice, and so on. The right approach to a problem is usually in an intermediate zone. But where? To answer this question, Aristotle says you should first look closely at the particular features and circumstances of a problem: try to understand all its nooks and crevices. Then, he says, you should rely on your judgment—on your experience, analysis, deliberation, and intuition—to decide what is right. In other words, the golden mean is where your judgment says it is.

As a result, different people, looking at the same problem or situation, can make different judgments about the right answer to a gray area problem. And Aristotle is comfortable with this—with one critical proviso. The individuals who make these judgments, he says, should have good character. They should be committed to and live by the classical virtues like honesty, courage, prudence, and justice. Aristotle's basic logic is this: character shapes judgment, and judgment resolves hard problems. Put differently, it is judgment, shaped by character, that says this is where we will draw the line, this is what we will and won't do, and this is what our organization will pursue or reject.[1]

The theme of the golden mean runs through a good deal of classical thinking. The Buddha advocated "the middle way."[2]

For Confucius, the admirable person resembles an archer who aims for the center of the target and reflects carefully when an arrow goes astray.[3] Maimonides warned, "If a man finds that his nature tends or is disposed to one of these extremes . . . he should turn back and improve, so as to walk in the way of good people, which is the right way."[4] Mohammed said the best choice was "the middle ground."[5]

If we turn from classical writers to the modern era, we find the same idea—that judgment and character are deeply intertwined—and we find this idea in the thinking of extraordinarily disparate individuals. For example, Friedrich Nietzsche was a brilliant, reclusive German poet and scholar, and one of the most influential philosophers of the modern era. He wrote about religion, power, and human nature, and one of his fundamental ideas was the impossibility of grasping reality. All we have, Nietzsche believed, is our own interpretation of reality. As he phrased it, "'This is *my* way, where is yours'—thus I answered those who asked me '*the* way.' For *the* way—that does not exist."[6]

A variation on Nietzsche's theme appears—astonishingly— in the opening pages of *My Years with General Motors*, the autobiography of Alfred P. Sloan. During the 1920s, Sloan forged the modern GM from a near-bankrupt hodgepodge of automotive companies. By the 1950s, under Sloan's leadership, GM had become the largest and most profitable company in history. Sloan pioneered approaches to strategy, organization, accounting, finance, and manufacturing that were adopted by countless other companies, and continue to shape organizations today.[7] He firmly believed in basing management decisions on facts and analysis. Yet, in his autobiography Sloan wrote, "The final act of business judgment is, of course, intuitive."[8]

Notice the last three words in this statement. Sloan—the brilliant, dedicated, lifelong analyst and systematizer—says that *intuition*, not facts or analysis, is the pivotal factor in making decisions. Notice also that Sloan says "of course." For him, the role of intuition was plain. His firm conviction was that, in the end, the final, decisive factor for making serious decisions is an intuitive judgment—a hard-to-pin-down fusion of a particular individual's experience, character, and perspective—that determines whether one course of action is, in the end, better than another.

Sloan's view is a humanist account of decision making. And, remarkably, it is a perspective that Sloan shared, not just with classical thinkers, but with the existentialists—the philosophers, novelists, diarists, and poets who are the humanists of our modern era. Some existentialists were deeply religious, others were atheists; some were abstract thinkers, others wrote plainly and concretely. In Europe, fifty years ago, many existentialist thinkers were searching intensely for answers to the deepest questions—about life and its meaning—in the aftermath of the terrible wars and unthinkable barbarism on European and Asian soil.

The existentialists understood the inevitability, finality, and burden of choice. They grasped what men and women with real responsibility in life know from experience. Choice and commitment are inevitable and inescapable, particularly in the face of fluid, complex, uncertain problems. Making these decisions is sometimes a heavy burden, sometimes a bracing challenge, and always a profoundly human task.

Intuition and judgment enable us to meet this challenge. In other words, the critical, final moment in making hard decisions is a partly conscious, partly unconscious melding of mind and heart, analysis and instinct. A well-respected senior executive described his own version of this approach to difficult decisions by saying, "I wouldn't go ahead with something just because my brain told me it was the right thing to do. I also had to feel it. If I didn't, I had to get my brain and my gut into harmony."

Practical Challenges

Despite its commanding legacy, the fifth question seems to have a significant or fatal flaw, especially if we think about it in everyday, concrete terms. Do we really want to rely heavily on whatever course of action a decision maker can live with? Do we really want the pivotal consideration on hard, high-stakes decisions to be whatever someone in charge somehow "feels" is right? What if this person is lazy, incompetent, sleazy, pervasively self-interested, corrupt, or just having a bad day?

Ernest Hemingway gave a clear example of this danger when he wrote, "About morals, I know only that what is moral is what you feel good after and what is immoral is what you feel bad after."[9] This suggests that hard decisions are basically personal, subjective, a matter of feelings and emotions, and hence arbitrary. It says that, if the great savages of history, like Hitler and Stalin, felt good about what they did, then they were moral.

Hemingway's view is profoundly challenging. It asks, in effect: What do we have to show for century after century of serious thinking about the right way to make hard decisions? The answer seems to be: not much. No single approach or school or theory has won out. All we have is a record of endless, sometimes brilliant, sometimes ponderous disputation. We can admire the intellectual fireworks, but we don't find a firm foundation we can stand on—and this is troubling. It suggests that men and women in positions of power have no objective principles to follow when they make final choices. A statement by the French existentialist Jean-Paul Sartre—"If God does not exist, all is permitted"—is a famous and disturbing version of this view.[10]

The fifth question also seems hazardous in a second way. It assumes we can actually know who we are. But do we? There are some very good reasons, which we can discover in the wisdom of ancient writers or by self-reflection, for thinking that it is very difficult, perhaps almost impossible, to know who we are. Self-understanding is a central humanist concern, and serious thinkers have grappled with it for millennia. The Oracle of Delphi in ancient Greece welcomed visitors with the command "Know thyself." This precept was etched in stone above the temple entrance, and it appears, again and again, in the works of a wide range of thinkers. But this advice is usually accompanied with warnings.

In *Poor Richard's Almanac,* for example, Benjamin Franklin wrote, "There are three things extremely hard: steel, a diamond, and to know one's self."[11] As we have seen, a great deal of sophisticated, contemporary research suggests that we don't even have stable, enduring selves—in so many situations, in laboratories, in real life, and in history—the power of situations has overwhelmed the "true selves" of most people. And a good deal of classic literature shows how often and how easily we betray whatever true self we have. Shakespeare described the problem in mocking tones in *Measure for Measure*, where he wrote:

> *But man, proud man,*
> *Dressed in a little brief authority,*
> *Most ignorant of what he's most assured,*
> *His glassy essence, like an angry ape*
> *Plays such fantastic tricks before high heaven*
> *As makes the angels weep.*[12]

These challenges to the fifth question seem to undermine the basic theme of this book: the idea that men and women should approach gray area issues as managers and resolve them as human beings. One challenge is that human beings can be distracted, ill informed, negligent, lazy, deeply self-interested, or outright evil. The other is that it can be very hard to understand who we really are and what we really care about. Perhaps the fifth question should simply be reserved for inspirational occasions, like patriotic events and commencement addresses.

But that isn't a real option. In one form or another, the fifth question is inescapable. When individuals or organizations face hard problems, the process of analysis has to come to an end. At some point, someone has to make a decision. And, if the facts and the framing are unclear, the person making the decision will have discretion. The decision will reflect this person's judgment and—as so many important thinkers have told us—their judgment will reflect, in significant ways, who they are and what they can live with. In short, for gray area issues, personal judgment is inevitable and decisive, and character inevitably shapes it—for well and ill.

Practical Guidance: Tempered Intuition

The practical guidance for the fifth question is surprising. It seems to depart, at least initially, from Alfred Sloan's view that intuition is the final and decisive step in making hard decisions. But that is because we sometimes see intuition as a little bird that alights on our shoulder and whispers the truth. This is a charming, but profoundly misleading notion—at least for managers facing gray areas. What they need and what Sloan recommended is intuition that has been tempered and tested, not spontaneous.

Tempered intuition requires a period of deliberation. That is the clear suggestion of familiar expressions like "turning something over in your mind." It is the rationale for the advice to "sleep on it" before making a decision. It is the reason that many of the great religious traditions recommend specific, often extended practices, like the *Spiritual Exercises of St. Ignatius of Loyola*, as preparation for life and its serious choices.[13] In other words, tempered intuition isn't instantaneous insight. It reflects a process of consideration, reflection, and deliberation in the mind and heart of the person who has to make a hard decision.

The practical guidance in this chapter is for the period just before you make a decision about a gray area problem. When time is short, this period may be brief, but often you have several days. Few important management decisions are made under acute time pressure, and good organizations and good managers make sure there is enough time for decisions that matter. And the reason, as before, involves process. For a final decision, however, the process that matters takes place in your mind and heart. And, fortunately, there are several steps you can rely on because, for centuries, they have guided the intuitive judgments of men and women facing hard decisions.

Get Off the Merry-Go-Round

Shakespeare's *Macbeth* is a dark, turbulent story of ambition, treachery, and moral collapse. So it is easy, while watching or reading the play, to overlook the three-word phrase in which Shakespeare distills a crucial piece of guidance—something Macbeth failed to follow in his headlong rush to disaster. The phrase is "the pauser, reason."[14]

The first step in testing and tempering your intuition is as much physical as intellectual or psychological. It is taking time out. This means you ending your conversations with others about the problem, closing the door, muting the electronics, and then looking out the window or gazing at the wall. It means finding a convenient and comfortable way for you to step back, if only temporarily and partially, from everything going on around you.

As Shakespeare emphasized, reason involves pausing—as do imagination, feelings, convictions, and the other elements of a tempered intuition. The first four questions and the humanist perspective they represent are crucial ways to slow down and look carefully at a situation or problem. And the deeper suggestion in Shakespeare's phrase is that those who haven't paused probably haven't reasoned or deliberated. They may instead be plunging ahead, missing important insights, courting danger, or doing damage, because they are the unwitting puppets of the emotions, drives, and biases compressed in their unexamined instincts.

Use All Five Questions and Don't Pick Your Favorite

There are two ways to view the long-standing and apparently permanent disagreement among serious thinkers about the right way to make hard decisions. One is the skeptical or cynical view. It sees the whole effort as the intellectual version of a circular firing squad: each way of thinking undermines and discredits the others, no single, sound approach emerges, and all we have left is disagreement and confusion. As a widely respected political theorist put it, "The substructure of the ethical world is a subject of deep and apparently unending controversy."[15]

The other approach is the one in this book: seeing these powerful arguments and their insights about decision making as a long and illuminating conversation about a reality—the essence of judgment and sound decisions—that is intrinsically multifaceted. There is no single, final, simple insight that comes in a nice little box with a bow on top. In this great conversation, no one view of ethics or decision making has won out—because human beings and our lives together are simply too varied, subtle, and complex. Each voice in the great conversation provides valuable, if partial insights for men and women facing difficult decisions. This is why William James, one of the founders of American pragmatism, wrote, "Facts are good, of course—give us lots of facts. Principles are good—give us plenty of principles."[16]

An old saying tells us that we see the world, not as it is, but as we are. In other words, thoughtful, intelligent people, looking at the same situation, will differ about what the situation is and what to do about it. The four questions are antidotes to the hazards of this reality. They can help us to some extent see the world as it actually is or at least see it as others see it. Sound deliberation counters the temptation to grasp hold of a single grand principle and use it to dominate other ways of thinking. This means viewing the five questions, not as majestic, final truths, but as useful, everyday tools. Carpenters work with toolboxes. They don't try to do everything with a saw or a screwdriver. The same, sensible approach works for the great humanist questions. This means desanctifying and demystifying them, seeing them as implements, and using them all.

This approach improves deliberation and judgment because the questions complement, correct, and strengthen each other. To see this, think about people you know. Some think naturally in terms of consequences, some feel strongly obligated by their duties, others are naturally or even disturbingly pragmatic, and some seem to embody, in what they say and do, the important values of a community or organization. Each of us has natural grooves in our thinking, and this can lead to problems. People who think only about consequences can trample on basic human duties. Pragmatism alone can be amoral or worse. And a preoccupation with the values that bind a group together can obscure serious consequences for people outside the group and strong duties to them.

The fifth question—What can I live with?—is dangerous if someone uses it as the *only* question, rather than the final question. That is because the first four questions serve, in effect, as border guards policing a territory. Within this territory, managers can trust themselves to make sound decisions—on the basis of their convictions, their judgment, and their sense of what is right for their organization in a particular set of circumstances. But the border guards limit this freedom. Its exercise can't impose significant hardships on others, violate basic duties, or ignore the values that define an organization. That is why the second piece of guidance for final reflection says to use all five of the questions, rather than rely on your favorite one.

Expect to Struggle

Notice how the fifth question is phrased. It doesn't ask about what is best or what is right. Instead, it suggests a more modest and realistic standard: simply being able to live with and accept a decision. Put differently, the fifth question recognizes that what managers have to struggle with are often questions like these: Which option am I least uncomfortable with? Which option will lead to the fewest regrets?

These questions reflect the basic nature of gray areas. Discomfort and misgivings come with the territory. Gray area problems have no easy answers. They involve hard choices and difficult trade-offs. And, even when managers do all they can to get these decisions right, they often have to live with troubling uncertainty about whether they made the right decision and whether their efforts will accomplish what they want. In a gray area, struggle is usually a sign of serious thought and effort.

For example, Alisha Wilson said she lost "a fair amount of sleep" as she tried to decide what to do about Kathy Thompson. Wilson's main concern was that whatever problem was causing Thompson's failure at work would also keep her from getting the help she needed after she lost her job. In the end, Wilson met with Thompson several times. The conversations were awkward because Wilson was walking a fine line between her duty to respect her assistant's privacy and the potentially dire consequences of simply terminating her. Wilson wanted to help Thompson but, as her boss, she felt she had no right to intrude into her employee's personal life.

Finally and reluctantly, Wilson told Thompson she was likely to lose her job and that she needed to look into getting long-term disability coverage before this happened. Thompson eventually followed this advice and, later on, Wilson helped her find an attorney to assist with the complicated application process, because Wilson didn't think Thompson could handle it on her own. However, despite all her efforts, Wilson was never sure she had done the right thing. Perhaps she pushed too hard; perhaps she didn't do enough. All Wilson knew for sure was that, several years later, no bad news about Thompson was circulating through the grapevine.

Two lessons about reflection and expectations emerge from this incident. One is that reflection on gray areas often means feeling anxiety, hesitating, going back and forth, and losing sleep. None of these reactions are signs of failure. In all likelihood, they show that someone really understands a situation, grasps what is at stake, and sees the challenges of resolving the problem. In other words, smooth sailing through a gray area means someone isn't paying attention or doesn't really understand what is going on.

The other lesson is that, with gray area problems, all you can sometimes hope for and struggle for is getting the process right. Alisha Wilson's only solid reassurance was that she had engaged in a long, honest process of trying to understand Kathy Thompson's problem and resolving it in a way she could live with. With others, she had worked through the full consequences of her options, the rights and duties at stake, the pragmatic limits on what she could do, and the norms of her organization. Wilson tried hard to get the process right, in hopes of getting the decision right.

What managers can reasonably expect in gray areas was described in *Cato*, an eighteenth-century drama that influenced and inspired several of the American founding fathers. At one point, the main character in the play, the Roman stoic Cato, tells one of his followers, "Tis not in mortals to command success, but we'll do more, Sempronius, we'll deserve it."[17]

Make a Trial Decision

At some point, deliberation has to come to an end and a manager has to make a final decision. This is probably the point at which Sloan's "intuition" plays a decisive role. A manager decides that some considerations matter more than others and then makes a decision that he or she can live with. But this raises a tricky problem. We have, in effect, two selves. One is our present self, who is making the decision, and the other is our future self, who will live with the decision. And there is strong evidence that we aren't very good at judging how our future self will react to decisions made by our present self.[18] So how can we know, with some decent degree of confidence, that we will actually be able to live with a decision?

One approach was suggested by one of the most widely respected leaders of ancient times, the Roman emperor and general, Marcus Aurelius. Marcus is remembered today for his battlefield victories, wise rule, and, above all, for the diary he kept. Late at night, he sat down by candlelight and wrote the observations and deliberations that came to be called *Meditations*. Readers often skim the beginning of this book. It seems to be little more than a list of people to whom Marcus is grateful—like the acknowledgments sections in books today. But skimming is a mistake. Marcus describes all the men and women who influenced his life. He tells us explicitly what virtues and skills he learned from each of them and, most important, he seems to view them as an invisible jury to which he holds himself accountable.

Following Marcus's example takes only a change in focus and a little imagination. Ask yourself, for example, how you would explain your gray area problem to someone you really respect and whose judgment really matters to you. How would you explain this decision to a manager or leader that you hold in high esteem or view as a role model? How do you think they would react? Would you feel comfortable with your explanation? How you would explain the problem and your way of handling it to a spouse, partner, or one of your children, or, if you are religious, to a priest, rabbi, imam, minister, or other religious guide?

What Marcus Aurelius suggested, almost two thousand years ago, has stood the test of time because it sets a demanding, complex, yet realistic standard for behavior. It is demanding because it makes personal accountability vivid and concrete by referring to specific individuals. It is complex because it is, simultaneously, an internal and external standard. Marcus refers to outsiders, but they are outsiders he has chosen and cares about, so they reflect his own sense of his best self. Finally, the standard is realistic and practical because it is a way of countering our biologically installed, often unconscious, innate talent for rationalization and self-deception. The aim of this exercise is to see your words, your thinking, your values, and your judgment from the outside, but against a standard—the judgment of people you really respect—that matters deeply to you.

The practical guidance for the fifth question is a way of finding *a* sound way to resolve a gray area issue, not *the* right way. Different managers will resolve gray area problems in different ways. Put in the same situation, they will weigh the consequences, duties, practicalities, and values differently, and take different approaches to resolving complex problems. This isn't because some managers are smarter or are better people. It is because every manager has his or her own sense of how the world works and what really matters. The fifth humanist question is a way of evoking this personal perspective on really hard decisions.

In the end, a sense you can live with a decision on a hard gray area problem may not come from a conviction that you have found the clear, right answer. In some gray area situations, all you can know with confidence is that you worked hard to get the process right. This means you approached the problem as responsible, serious manager, you worked with others to pin down the crucial facts, tried to make sound judgments about important uncertainties, and thought hard about the right ways to analyze the problem. And then you deliberated carefully before making a decision. This is the kind of assurance Aaron Feuerstein had in mind when he was asked what he wanted on his tombstone. After a long pause, he said simply, "He did his damnedest."[19]

Make the Decision, Explain It, and Move Ahead

At some point, of course, managers have to make decisions about gray area problems and move ahead with implementation. And they have to explain these decisions to other people, clearly and persuasively. This final step is, in some ways, the most important. Management is an art, but not the kind you see in museums. It is a performance art, and the best managers are skilled at reaching their audiences: the people their decisions will affect and whose cooperation they need.

When you have to communicate your decision on a gray area issue, the five questions can be very useful. Each of these long-standing, deep, powerful perspectives on hard choices is, in effect, a radio frequency on which you can broadcast a clear signal. You can say, for example, that you have thought hard about a decision and have done what you believe is best for everyone who will be affected. Or you can say you have thought long and hard, and your decision meets basic duties. Or you can say that, after serious thought, you have chosen the best of the options that were realistic and practical. Or you can say that your decision best expresses, as you see it, the values that define your organization.

None of the questions, used this way, is a magic wand. You have to do the analysis and fill in the blanks. This means explaining—relying on facts, analysis, and judgment—why you believe that consequences or duties or practicalities or defining norms lead in a particular direction. Quite often, to be credible and convincing, you also have to explain the process you relied on to reach your decision. But all these explanations can be strongly amplified by framing them in terms of the humanist fundamentals.

In fact, one way to prepare an explanation of a tough decision is to write it down, briefly and clearly. One reason to do this is that writing compels clarity, which is crucial to approaching a problem like a manager. As the historian David McCullough put it, "Writing is thinking. To write well is to think clearly. That's why it's so hard."[20] Another reason is that writing is a form of personal commitment—which is crucial to making decisions as a human being. That is the insight behind the memorable statement of nineteenth-century author Guy de Maupassant: "Dark words on white paper bare the soul."[21]

Specifically, look at the gray area you face and try to answer each of the great humanist questions. Try to be brief and clear: in other words, try to cut to the essentials. As you see it, what are the most important possible consequences? Which duties do you believe are central? Which pragmatic considerations really concern you? What community norms do you believe you and your organization must respect?

What happens after you have made a final decision about a gray area problem and communicated your decision as effectively as you can? Part of the answer is obvious. You have to work hard on implementation. You may also find that your decision isn't "final." Gray areas are uncharted terrain, so you shouldn't be surprised to encounter resistance, surprises, disappointments, and unexpected opportunities. You may also find that your "final" decision needs adjustment or even significant changes, once the implementation starts. And, despite your best efforts, you may find that you need to continue hammering away to communicate your decision clearly. It is often very difficult to get a clear signal through the ambient noise inside organizations.

Most important, once you have resolved one gray area issue, you have to get ready to handle the next one—and the one after that—because gray area decisions are the core of management work. When Jim Mullen reflected on the Tysabri episode, he said, "All the stuff that's black and white already gets decided before it comes to the CEO. If the black-and-white stuff arrives in my office, there's something wrong with the organization. What arrives in my office is all the gray stuff."[22]

Mullen is saying that, once you become a manager, the messy, high-stakes problems become a central part of your job. And, when you go home after work, you don't escape the challenge of gray areas. Men and women who take on real responsibility, at work or elsewhere in life, find there is no way to dispel all the gray. This is why the five questions are so important. They are a valuable toolkit for the times when you face a hard decision, but they are important in another, deeper way. The five questions, taken together, offer a basic philosophy or worldview to men and women who take their responsibilities seriously.

Ethically Sensitive Pragmatism

This book has sketched what could be called a working philosophy for managers, based on five important humanist perspectives. This philosophy doesn't consist of abstract concepts or binding principles. It is a disposition, an attitude, a habit of mind, and an implicit worldview. It is a distinctive way of sizing up gray area issues, analyzing them carefully, grappling with their full, human complexity, and then—and only then—making final decisions. This worldview says, in essence, that successful, responsible leaders are ethically sensitive pragmatists. This view of management can be summarized in two simple statements.

First, managers facing hard problems have to be sensitive to a range of fundamental human concerns—about consequences for other people, about their basic duties, about the hard realities of getting things done, about constitutive community values, and about what really matters to them personally. These fundamental concerns are ethics in its fullest sense. We often think about ethics in terms of do's and don'ts, but the five questions raise deeper concerns. They are profound ways of asking what really matters in life, in communities, and in decisions.

The working philosophy presented in this book doesn't enshrine any of the questions or claim that one dominates the others. Nor does it dismiss these perspectives because none of them provides ultimate answers. Ethically sensitive pragmatism sees the ideas underlying each of the five questions as valuable windows on human complexity. This is why leaders who follow this approach work hard to be sensitive and responsive to a range of fundamental human considerations. The British explorer, linguist, and polymath Richard Francis Burton was a practical man with a poetic gift. He captured this first aspect of ethically sensitive pragmatism when he wrote, "All faith is false, all faith is true: truth is the shattered mirror strewn in myriad bits; while each believes his own little bit the whole to own."[23]

Ethical sensitivity accepts and respects the many ways in which human intelligence, imagination, and experience have tried to understand how to make complex, uncertain decisions in the right way. As a working philosophy, ethically sensitive pragmatism means grappling with the varied, inevitable, and deep complexities—technical, human, social, and moral—of gray area decisions. This is why sensitivity, awareness, flexibility, and responsiveness are so important to this view of the world.

The second basic statement that describes ethically sensitive pragmatism says that, as a manager, you have work to do. You have to resolve gray area issues in ways that are realistic and practical. This means getting the process right—when you approach the problem as a manager and when you ultimately resolve it as a human being. But process has to end. At some point, you have to say to others, clearly and plainly: "This is my decision, this is why I made it, and this is what we are going to do." Doing this well means following the long-standing practical guidance embedded in the five questions: looking broadly and deeply, awakening your moral imagination and relying on it, testing your plans and yourself for resilience against surprises and politics, and really understanding the stories that give meaning to your organization.

Of course, the conventional wisdom says that a pragmatic, get-the-job-done approach undermines sensitivity to serious human concerns. And this is often true. Pragmatism can simply mean putting on blinders and setting the ethical niceties aside. But ethically sensitive pragmatists approach this challenge differently. They work hard and often struggle to find ways through gray areas that work for their organizations, their teams, and themselves and, at the same time, are sensitive to serious human concerns.

Ethically sensitive pragmatists accept complexity, ethical and practical. They also embrace this complexity—not because this makes decisions easier, but because it makes them better. They believe that, by putting decisions in their full, realistic, human context, they raise the chances they will really understand what is at stake when they face hard decisions and will then have the right foundation for making good decisions.

This was one of the critical lessons that David Lilienthal, one of the most widely experienced and successful executives of the last century, drew from his career. During the 1930s, Lilienthal helped design and then led the Tennessee Valley Authority when it was constructing a vast, multistate network of dams and electrical infrastructure. In the 1940s, he helped create and then ran the Atomic Energy Commission, at a time when this new technology promised to transform human life and threatened to extinguish it. Then, during the 1950s, Lilienthal founded an engineering consulting firm.

For decades, Lilienthal kept a detailed diary in which he reflected on his work and his life. Late in his career, Lilienthal looked back at his wide experience and summarized his view of managers' work. "The managerial life," he wrote, "is the broadest, the most demanding, and by all odds the most comprehensive and subtle of all human activities."[24]

For Lilienthal, management was a way of life, not just a job or career. And successful management was, as he saw it, a "humanist art."[25] This is why responsible managers should work hard to make sure that, when they face hard, complex issues, their decisions rest on the deep-sunk pylons of consequences, basic duties, practical realities, defining community values—and on their abiding, personal sense of what really matters in life.

Humanism

There is a vast literature on humanism and many defini-
tions of the term. Moreover, some scholars have argued that
the term has had so many meanings that it is "indefinable."[1]
Hence, this book uses the term in a specific way and it draws
on two perspectives. One consists of survey articles by scholars with deep expertise on humanism. The other, inevitably,
is the viewpoint of the author. This has been shaped, in part,
by many years of reading and teaching about Machiavelli; a
long-standing interest in Michel de Montaigne, his essays,
and the many interpretations of them; and the ideas and
intellectual viewpoint of the great contemporary humanist
and historian of ideas, Isaiah Berlin.

This book interprets humanism as:

1. *A Renaissance movement.* It prized the recovery of ancient Greek and Roman learning, as well as new scientific developments.

2. *A loose body of kindred ideas.* Humanists generally celebrate freedom, curiosity, openness, the possibility of progress, a conviction that people can live well without metaphysical or scientific certainty, and a cosmopolitan curiosity about all the many ways in which people live and have lived. The famous statement by Terrence, the ancient Roman playwright—"Nothing human is alien to me" —is a strong undercurrent in humanist thinking.

3. *A way of learning.* Humanists give a privileged position to history, politics, ethics, poetry, and rhetoric. These, they believed, enable human beings to make the best use of their freedom and make wise choices about their lives.

4. *A preference for the active rather than the contemplative life.* An initial phase of humanism, in fourteenth-century Italy, placed great confidence in the capacity of human beings to shape the world and determine the course of their lives. A century later, Montaigne and Machiavelli were more skeptical. Montaigne's essays, which were perhaps unprecedented in human history, revealed the complexities, fluidity, subtleties, and treacheries of the human psyche. Machiavelli offered a parallel view of political life.

5. *A complex view of religion and religious institutions.*
The Renaissance humanists rejected the medieval
view that long-standing institutions like the Catholic
Church, the Holy Roman Empire, and the feudal system were all part of a cosmic order that human beings
had to accept and could not change. At the same time,
the Renaissance humanists—unlike some contemporary groups that call themselves "humanist"—did
not necessarily oppose religion or endorse atheism or
agnosticism, and instead advocated religious tolerance.
Some Renaissance humanists believed that all religions were ways of expressing the same fundamental
insights about the spiritual nature of the universe.
Others believed that Christianity did not replace or
reject the wisdom of ancient philosophy, but simply
brought it to fulfillment.

6. *A historical rather than a theoretical way of understanding
human beings, their lives, and their important decisions.*
For humanists, what really matters is understanding
context, with all its nuances and particulars: the actual
time and place in which events occurred and decisions had to be made, as well as the personalities and
motives of individuals making decisions and shaping
events.

The interpretation of humanism in this book draws on:

Baron, Hans. "15th-Century Civilization and the
Renaissance." In *The New Cambridge Modern History*, vol. 1,

The Renaissance, 1493–1520, 50–75. Cambridge: Cambridge University Press, 1992.

Berlin, Isaiah. "The Originality of Machiavelli." In *Against the Current: Essays in the History of Ideas*, edited by Henry Hardy and Roger Hausheer, 25–79. Princeton, NJ: Princeton University Press, 2001.

Cassirer, Ernst, Paul Oskar Kristeller, and John Herman Randall Jr., eds. *The Renaissance Philosophy of Man: Petrarca, Valla, Ficino, Pico, Pomponazzi, Vives*. Chicago: University of Chicago Press, 1956.

Davies, Tony. *Humanism*. New York: Routledge, 2008.

Gray, John. *Isaiah Berlin: An Interpretation of His Thoughts*. Princeton, NJ: Princeton University Press, 2013.

Greenblatt, Stephen. *The Swerve: How the World Became Modern*. New York: W. W. Norton & Company, 2012.

Ignatieff, Michael. *Isaiah Berlin: A Life*. New York: Metropolitan Books, 1998.

Kolenda, Konstantin. "Humanism." In *The Cambridge Dictionary of Philosophy*, edited by Robert Audi, 396–397. Cambridge: Cambridge University Press, 1999.

Kraye, Jill, ed. *The Cambridge Companion to Renaissance Humanism*. Cambridge: Cambridge University Press, 1996.

Kristeller, Paul Oskar. "Humanism." In *The Cambridge History of Renaissance Philosophy*, edited by Charles B.

Schmidt and Quentin Skinner, 113–140. Cambridge: Cambridge University Press, 1988.

Machiavelli, Niccolò. *The Prince*. New York: Penguin Classics, 2003. First published 1532.

de Montaigne, Michel. *The Complete Essays of Montaigne*. Translated by Donald Frame. Redwood City, CA: Stanford University Press, 1958.

APPENDIX B

Human Nature, Evolution, and Ethics

More than two millennia ago, Aristotle suggested that human beings shared a common nature—an idea that is now the focus of intense study and controversy. Aristotle is known, of course, as a pioneering philosopher, ethicist, and political thinker, but he was also the first important biologist and zoologist in the West, and his famous definition of human beings draws on his scientific background. What he said, with the power of simplicity, is that human beings are political or social animals.[1]

The usual practice for philosophers, sociologists, and other thinkers is to focus on the political and social aspects

153

of human nature, but Aristotle also emphasized that human beings are animals. In other words, we are creatures and, like other creatures, we have certain built-in traits and tendencies. These aren't like software code—they don't program us and determine what we think and do. Instead they incline us or spring-load us to think, feel, and act in certain ways. To a significant degree, they make us what we are.

This way of thinking makes some people uncomfortable, because it seems to reduce human beings to mere animals and ignores our intellectual, artistic, social, technological, and spiritual achievements. But that is hardly the case. The argument is not that evolution and genetics shape all or most of what we do or that our instincts and drives are fundamentally animalistic. Thomas Aquinas, the great Catholic theologian, wrote, "We do not merely have, but are our bodies." Aquinas also wrote, "Since the soul is part of the body of a human being, the soul is not the whole human being and my soul is not I."[2]

If some version of Aristotle's view is correct, it may help explain why certain ways of thinking about hard problems have engaged the best minds and hearts, in so many different cultures and eras, and why our everyday thinking about hard decisions also reflects these perspectives. The reason is that certain ways of grappling with hard problems strengthen the cooperative tendencies that helped the human species survive and help overcome other innate tendencies that reduce the chance of survival.

Should we accept Aristotle's view? His stature, as one of the most important thinkers in the Western tradition, means we should take his ideas seriously, but we shouldn't accept an idea simply because Aristotle—or, for that matter, any important thinker—happens to assert it. And, if we look beyond Aristotle's thinking, we find strong support for the idea of a common human nature in contemporary evolutionary theory.

Evolutionary theory asks what capabilities, traits, and tendencies would have helped human creatures or our prehuman ancestors survive the rigors of natural selection. Creatures that shared these traits would have been more likely to survive, reproduce, and evolve into us. Evolutionary science today draws on psychology, biology, genetics, anthropology, and other disciplines to sketch plausible pictures of social practices and ways of thinking and acting that might have enabled our distant ancestors to survive and evolve in our direction.

The broad argument is that the early humans and prehumans who survived and evolved into us did so because they had inclinations to cooperate with each other. The groups with more "cooperators" were more likely to survive—because their members could work together to solve the basic problems of survival—protecting their young, finding and storing food, fending off predators, winning battles against other human groups. Our common human nature—as social animals—reflects the traits or premoral instincts that help our distant ancestors meet and surmount common human challenges.

The view that human beings may have some innate cooperative instincts runs counter to the classic, reductionist views of evolution. It describes natural selection as, in essence, an endless process of remorseless struggle that pits every creature against every creature. Alfred Lord Tennyson's famous phrase—"nature red in tooth and claw"—summarizes this way of thinking about evolution.

If there is some common human nature, what is it? What form does it take? Here, once again, evolutionary theory—as well as many philosophical and religious traditions, along with psychological theory—point toward the same broad answer. The basic idea is that the human creature is flawed, divided, and torn. We are pulled back and forth between benevolent, altruistic, and admirable impulses and aggressive, vicious, predatory ones. This theme is a bright thread that runs vividly, not just through evolutionary theory and religious traditions, but also through great literature, serious historical works, the close observation of everyday life, and personal introspection.

What does this have to do with ethics? During the last two decades, scholars and scientists from a wide range of disciplines have been focused intensely on understanding the relationship between human nature—to the extent there is a common human nature—and human evolution. Others have focused more sharply and tried to discern relationships between evolution, as it is now understood, and the widespread, almost universal practice of developing ethical norms. An emerging answer is that a cooperative, perhaps partially altruistic disposition—which ethical theory articulates in various ways—helped to express and channel our narrowly self-interested and predatory instincts and enabled the human species to survive and reproduce successfully.

The foregoing account of the relationship between evolution and human nature draws on the following works:

Boehm, Christopher. *Moral Origins: The Evolution of Virtue, Altruism, and Shame.* New York: Basic Books, 2012.

Dawkins, Richard. *The Selfish Gene.* Oxford: Oxford University Press, 1976.

Flack, J. C., and Frans B. M. de Waal. "Any Animal Whatever: Darwinian Building Blocks of Morality in Monkeys and Apes." In *Evolutionary Origin of Morality: Cross-Disciplinary Perspectives*, edited by Leonard D. Katz, 1–29. Bowling Green, OH: Imprint Academic, 2002.

Kitcher, Philip. *The Ethical Project.* Cambridge, MA: Harvard University Press, 2011.

Krygier, Martin. *Philip Selznick: Ideals in the World.* Stanford, CA: Stanford University Press, 2012.

Kupperman, Joel. *Theories of Human Nature.* Cambridge, MA: Hackett Publishing Company, 2010.

MacIntyre, Alisdair. *Dependent Rational Animals: Why Human Beings Need the Virtues.* Chicago: Open Court Press, 1999.

Pinker, Stephen. *The Blank Slate: The Modern Denial of Human Nature.* New York: Penguin Books, 2003.

Stevenson, Leslie, and David L. Haberman. *Ten Theories of Human Nature*, chapter 11. Oxford: Oxford University Press, 2008.

Alfred Lord Tennyson. "In Memoriam A. H. H." 1850. http://www.portablepoetry.com/poems/alfredlord_tennyson/in_memoriam_ahh_____. Html. The phrase about nature comes from Canto 56, which refers to man:

> *Who trusted God was love indeed*
> *And love Creation's final law*
> *Tho' Nature, red in tooth and claw*
> *With ravine, shriek'd against his creed.*

Wilson, E. O. *The Social Conquest of Earth.* New York: Liveright Publishers, 2013.

Wilson, James Q. *The Moral Sense.* New York: Simon & Schuster, 1997.

NOTES

Chapter One

1. Lawrence J. Henderson, quoted in *On the Social System: Selected Writings*, ed. Bernard Barber (Chicago: University of Chicago Press, 1970), 67.

Chapter Two

1. Former Marine Corps Lieutenant Patrick Abell, personal communication, May 21, 2014.

2. Nitin Nohria and Thomas R. Piper, "Malden Mills (A) (Abridged)," Case no. 9-410-083 (Boston: Harvard Business School, 2010).

3. Rebecca Leung, "The Mensch of Malden Mills," *60 Minutes*, July 3, 2003, http://www.cbsnews.com/news/the-mensch-of-malden-mills/.

4. The poem is by Samuel Taylor Coleridge. Mill quotes Coleridge in the fifth chapter of his autobiography, which describes his depression and recovery (John Stuart Mill, *The Autobiography of John Stuart Mill* [1873; Stockbridge, MA: Liberal Arts Press, 1957], 134).

5. John Stuart Mill, *Utilitarianism* (1861; New York: Hacket Publishing Company, 2002), 14. Mill's biographer Nicholas Capaldi offers this interpretation of Mill's statement: happiness requires "the general cultivation of nobleness of character" and it encompasses "the comparatively humble sense of pleasure and freedom from pain" and "a higher meaning of rendering life such as human beings with highly

developed faculties have." See Nicholas Capaldi, *John Stuart Mill: A Biography* (Cambridge: Cambridge University Press, 2004), 261–265.

6. This quotation appears in Chris Fraser, "Mohism," *The Stanford Encyclopedia of Philosophy*, ed. Edward N. Zalta (Fall 2012 edition), http://plato.stanford.edu/archives/fall2012/entries/mohism/.

7. A full explanation of this doctrine is Carine Defroot, "Are the Three 'Jian Ai' Chapters about Universal Love?" in *The Mozi as an Evolving Text*, ed. Carine Defoort and Nicollas Standaert (Leiden/ Boston: Brill, 2013), 35–68.

8. David Hume, *An Enquiry Concerning the Principles of Morals*, ed. Tom L. Beauchamp (Oxford: Oxford University Press, 1998), 74.

9. The standard work on this topic is Philip E. Tetlock, *Expert Political Judgment: How Good Is It? How Can We Know?* (Princeton, NJ: Princeton University Press, 2009).

10. Robert K. Merton, "The Unanticipated Consequences of Purposive Social Action," *American Sociological Review* 1, no. 6 (December 1936): 894–904.

11. For an introduction to the challenges of intuitive decision making and recent psychological research on this topic, see Malcolm Gladwell, *Blink* (New York: Back Bay Books/Little, Brown & Co, 2005). The magisterial work on these topics is Daniel Kahneman, *Thinking, Fast and Slow* (New York: Farrar, Straus and Giroux, 2011). Others studies include Timothy D. Wilson, *Strangers to Ourselves: Discovering the Adaptive Unconscious* (Cambridge, MA: Belknap Press of Harvard University Press, 2002); Jonathan Haidt, *The Happiness Hypothesis: Finding Modern Truth in Ancient Wisdom* (New York: Basic Books, 2006); Richard H. Thaler and Cass R. Sunstein, *Nudge: Improving Decisions about Health, Wealth, and Happiness* (New Haven, CT: Yale University Press, 2008); Steven Pinker, *How the Mind Works* (New York: W.W. Norton & Company, 1997); Steven Pinker, *The Blank Slate: The Modern Denial of Human Nature* (New York: Viking, 2002); Max H. Bazerman and Ann E. Tenbrunsel, *Blind Spots: Why We Fail to Do What's Right and What to Do about It* (Princeton, NJ: Princeton University Press, 2011); and Francesca Gino, *Sidetracked: Why Our Decisions Get Derailed, and How We Can Stick to the Plan* (Boston: Harvard Business Review Press, 2013). The practical implications of the research described in these books are presented in detail in the May 2015 issue of *Harvard Business Review*.

12. See Shai Danziger, Jonothan Levav, and Liora Avnaim-Pesso, "Extraneous Factors in Judicial Decisions," *Proceedings of the National Academy of Science* 108, no. 17 (2012): 6889–6892.

13. This phrase appears in Pinker, *How the Mind Works*, 58.

14. Douglas Stanglin, "Oprah: A Heavenly Body?" *U.S. News and World Report*, March 27, 1987. A number of studies are consistent with this finding; see, for example, Nicholas Epley and David Dunning, "Feeling 'Holier Than Thou': Are Self-Serving Assessments Produced by Errors in Self- or Social Prediction?" *Journal of Personality and Social Psychology* 79, no. 6 (2000): 861–875.

15. Constantine Sedikides, Rosie Meek, Mark D. Alicke, and Sarah Taylor, "Behind Bars but Above the Bar: Prisoners Consider Themselves More Prosocial than Non-prisoners," *British Journal of Social Psychology* (2014).

16. This bias is a decades-old focus of psychological research. See Virginia S. Kwan, Oliver P. John, David A. Kenny, Michael H. Bond, and Richard W. Robins, "Reconceptualizing Individual Differences in Self-Enhancement Bias: An Interpersonal Approach," *Psychological Review* 3, no. 1 (January 2004): 94–110.

17. Bickel wrote this as part of a critique of US decision making on the war in Vietnam. The full passage reads, "Watergate was the latest assault, the only one which was at once vicious and powerful, the latest assault in an age of assaultive politics. We cannot survive a politics of moral attack. We must resume the politics of Burke's computing principle. The denominations to be computed are very often moral, to be sure, but few if any are absolute, few if any imperative. And the highest morality almost always is the morality of process." See Alexander Bickel, *The Morality of Consent* (New Haven, CT: Yale University Press, 1975), 123.

18. More than forty years ago, noted leadership scholar Leonard Sayles wrote an article that anticipated the preoccupation of recent decades with leadership, rather than management. See Leonard Sayles, "Whatever Happened to Management?—or Why the Dull Stepchild?," *Business Horizons*, April 1970, 25. Despite Sayles's question and warning, a long series of articles distinguished managers and leaders and valorized the latter. A classic article in this vein was Abraham Zaleznik, "Managers and Leaders: Are They Different?," *Harvard Business Review*,

May–June 1977. Zaleznik argues that managers and leaders work and think in very different ways, typically because of profound differences in childhood and early life experiences. A year later, a classic book on leadership by James McGregor Burns argued that the work of leaders was "transformational," while managers performed "transactional" tasks (*Leadership* [New York: Harper Perennial Classic Books, 2011]).

19. See, for example, Robin S. Doak, *The March on Washington: Uniting Against Racism* (New York: Compass Point Books, 2007), 35–63.

20. The examples of the nurse and the firefighter and the general description of this approach to making decisions are drawn from Gary A. Klein, Judith Orasanu, and Roberta Calderwood, *Decision Making in Action: Models and Methods* (Norwood, NJ: Ablex Publishing Co, 1993).

21. Scholars in many fields have tried to understand and describe more precisely how these "naturalistic" decisions are made, and some philosophers and even a few conceptually inclined managers have joined this effort. For an overview and a distinctive perspective on these issues, see John Shotter and Haridimos Tsoukas, "Performing Phronesis: On the Way to Engaged Judgment," *Management Learning* (August 2014): 377–396.

22. Jane Austen, *Pride and Prejudice* (1813; New York: Charles Scribner's Sons, 1918), 16.

23. Bayes is generally credited with the invention of decision theory based on probabilities, but some trace its origins to Renaissance polymath Gerolamo Cardano, who wrote a book on gambling, which he relied on for his living, that showed readers how to use probability estimates and also gave them detailed suggestions on how to cheat.

24. This is the perhaps most basic account and application of Bayes's theorem. Books on decision theory show its full power and complexity. A clear explanation of a more advanced approach than this one is Nate Silver, *The Signal and Noise* (New York: Penguin Press, 2012), 243–249. A broader, introductory book on decision making under uncertainty is Reid Hastie and Robyn Dawes, *Rational Choice in an Uncertain World* (Los Angeles: Sage Publications, 2010).

25. Recent laboratory studies suggest that framing ethical dilemmas in terms of what *could* be done rather than what *should* be done leaves or can

lead to the generation of a wider range of options and more creative and practical ways of resolving a dilemma. See Ting Zhang, Francesca Gino, and Joshua D. Margolis, "Does 'Could' Lead to Good? Toward a Theory of Moral Insight" (working paper, Harvard Business School, June 2014).

26. Tyler Cowen, *Average Is Over* (New York: Penguin, 2013), 98–110.

27. Madeleine Pelner Cosman and Linda C. Jones, *Handbook to Life in the Medieval World* (New York: Infobase Publishing, 2008), 347.

28. Robin Mejia, "Red Team Versus Blue Team: How to Run an Effective Simulation," *CSO Daily*, March 25, 2008, http://www.csoonline.com/article/2122440/emergency-preparedness/red-team-versus-blue-team--how-to-run-an-effective-simulation.html.

29. Doris Kearns Goodwin, *Team of Rivals: The Political Genius of Abraham Lincoln* (New York: Simon and Schuster, 2012).

30. Just what Stalin said and whether he actually said anything along these lines are matters of some contention. See, for example, http://quoteinvestigator.com/2010/05/21/death-statistic/.

Chapter Three

1. David McCullough, *Truman* (New York: Simon & Schuster, 2003), 555.

2. These natural duties, which seem to spring from the nature of human beings, can be defined and justified succinctly:

> Natural duties are "moral requirements which apply to all men [and women] irrespective of status or of acts performed . . .
> owed by all persons to all others" (Simmons 1979, 13). It is plausible to suppose that the fundamental or basic justification of why we have natural duties is the intrinsic nature of persons, i.e., the intrinsic nature of those to whom the duties are owed (moral patients). For example, consider my duty to tell the person sitting next to me at a bar that Joe Schmoe slipped poison into her drink. It may seem that I am morally required to tell only a limited class of people that someone has put poison into their drink, namely, the class consisting of the person sitting next to me right now whose drink is such

that I know that it is poisoned. However, the fundamental or basic justification for my having that duty is the nature of the person to whom the duty is owed . . . she is rational, or sentient, or [substitute your preferred characterization of a moral patient]—and her nature is sufficient to ground.

See Diane Jeske, "Special Obligations," *Stanford Encyclopedia of Philosophy*, ed. Edward N. Zalta (Spring 2014 edition), http://plato.stanford.edu/archives/spr2014/entries/special-obligations/.

3. Moritz Kronenberg, *Kant: Sein Leben und Seine Lehre* (Munich: C. H. Bedsche Buchverhandlung, 1904), 133.

4. An alternative way of reaching the same conclusion is presented in Larry Siedentop, *Inventing the Individual: The Origins of Western Liberalism* (Cambridge, MA: Belknap Press, 2014). Siedentop argues against the conventional view that liberalism arose in opposition to established religion and traces the origin of liberal conceptions of the individual to early religious thinkers.

5. *Catechism of the Catholic Church* (Vatican: Liberia Editrice Vaticana, 2000), article 1, paragraph 6, line 357. This type of argument, in its broadest terms, is called *status theory*. Philosopher Warren Quinn summarizes this approach: "A person is constituted by his body and his mind. They are parts or aspects of him. For that very reason, it is fitting that he have primary say over what may be done to them—not because such an arrangement best promotes overall human welfare, but because any arrangement that denied him that say would be a grave indignity. In giving him this authority, morality recognizes his existence as an individual with ends of his own—an independent being. Since that is what he is, he deserves this recognition." See Warren Quinn, *Morality and Action* (Cambridge, UK: Cambridge University Press, 1993), 170.

Many important thinkers who emphasize the centrality of human rights have been atheists and agnostics, and they have other strong reasons for their views. Some argue that human beings have rights because we are rational, conscious beings. Libertarians start with the premise that we essentially "own" our bodies and hence have rights to do what we want with and through them. Others believe that individual rights originate in a basic social contract that sets the terms for our political and social life.

In addition, the logic of consequences discussed in chapter 2 also provides a strong rationale for rights. What would society be like if individuals did not have a sense of basic security about their lives and their possessions? The likely answer came from the seventeenth-century political philosopher Thomas Hobbes, who said we would then live in a horrific state of nature, swept up in a "war of all against all." Hobbes used a phrase of the ancient Romans—"homo homini lupus"—to describe life without basic security: human beings would prey on each other like wolves. To avoid this, humans create social and political institutions. These institutions stipulate rights and duties, and they serve as bulwarks against barbarity.

6. Cicero, *On Duties* (Salt Lake City, Utah: Stonewell Press, 2013).

7. This quotation appears in Pierre Hadot, *The Inner Citadel: The Meditations of Marcus Aurelius*, (Cambridge, MA: Harvard University Press, 2001), 211. Hadot argues that stoicism is the ultimate origin of the Western emphasis on the absolute value of the human person.

8. This perspective isn't restricted to contemporary evolutionary theorists. Adam Smith, writing long before Charles Darwin, observed that "how selfish soever man may be supposed, there are evidently some principles in his nature which interested him in the fortune of others and render their happiness necessary to him, so he derives nothing from it except the pleasure of seeing it . . . by the imagination we place ourselves in his situation . . . we in turn as it were, into his body and become in some measure the same person with him." See Adam Smith, *The Theory of Moral Sentiments* (1759; New York: Penguin Classics, 2010), 2.

9. Stanford University historian Lynn Hunt asks how human rights became "self-evident truths" during the late 1700s and early 1800s. This was a remarkable development because slaveholding, torture, and the widespread subjugation of women had been accepted facts of everyday life. So what changed? Why did these practices begin to recede? After all, for centuries on end, they seemed to be permanent features of human existence.

Hunt's answer is the rise of popular media and mass media. Inexpensive novels and newspapers enabled more and more people in Europe and the nascent United States to learn—in compelling physical, psychological, and emotional detail—about the experiences of victims of oppression. People who had never been tortured or enslaved or suffered in extreme poverty read vivid direct accounts of how other people

Notes

experienced these conditions. This understanding triggered empathy. Readers intuited, emotionally rather than intellectually, that something was profoundly wrong about these practices. It was a short step from thinking these practices would be wrong for people like themselves to thinking they were wrong for everyone. See Lynn Hunt, *Inventing Human Rights: A History* (New York: W. W. Norton & Company, Inc., 2007).

10. The British philosopher Bernard Williams coined this phrase to summarize a basic critique of highly rationalistic approaches to ethical decisions. See Bernard Williams, *Moral Luck* (Cambridge, UK: Cambridge University Press, 1982), 17–18.

11. Kwame Anthony Appiah, *Cosmopolitanism: Ethics in a World of Strangers* (New York: W. W. Norton & Co., 2010), 52.

12. This account of the Tysabri problem is based primarily on Joshua D. Margolis and Thomas J. DeLong, "Antegren: A Beacon of Hope," Case no. 9-408-025 (Boston: Harvard Business School, 2007).

13. Leif Wenar, "Rights," *Stanford Encyclopedia of Philosophy*, ed. Edward N. Zalta (Fall 2011 edition), http://plato.stanford.edu/archives/fall2011/entries/rights/. A parallel problem appears in national constitutions. Most acknowledge some basic rights, but the range runs from New Zealand, whose constitution provides for no fundamental rights, to Bolivia's, which specifies eighty-eight basic rights. For a detailed comparison of political constitutions, see the Comparative Constitutions project at http://comparativeconstitutionsproject.org/ccp-rankings/.

14. John M. Darley and C. Daniel Batson, "From Jerusalem to Jericho: A Study of Situational and Dispositional Variables in Helping Behavior," *Journal of Personality Social Psychology* 27 (1973): 100–108.

15. Gerald E. Myers, *William James* (New Haven, CT: Yale University Press, 1986), 31.

16. For an extended discussion of the argument made in the two preceding paragraphs—that managers in the United States do not have and should not have a legal duty to maximize shareholder value—see, for example, Bruce Hay, Robert Stavins, and Richard Vietor, eds., *Environmental Protection and the Social Responsibility of Firms* (Washington, DC: Resources for the Future, 2005), 13–76; and Lynn Stout, *The Shareholder Value Myth: How Putting Shareholders First*

Harms Investors, Corporations, and the Public (San Francisco: Berrett-Koehler Publishers, 2012).

17. A leading legal scholar wrote in 2013:

> The flexible legal framework that enables the founding, growth, and organizational change of business firms allows for a wide range of choices of values that firms may embrace, as well as a wide range of choice about what specific goods and services are produced and how they are produced and sold. Nothing in the basic legal framework of business firms mandates a particular orientation to making money over all other possible values. Instead, the decentralized legal framework that exists in most parts of the world allows for a number of different kinds of firms to develop with mixtures of profit and nonprofit value orientation.

See Eric Orts, *Business Persons: Legal Theory of the Firm* (Oxford: Oxford University Press, 2013), 221.

18. An elaboration of this argument, as well as a description of the context of Tim Cook's comments, is Steve Denning, "Why Tim Cook Doesn't Care About 'The Bloody ROI,'" Forbes.com, March 7, 2014, http://www.forbes.com/sites/stevedenning/2014/03/07/why-tim-cook-doesnt-care-about-the-bloody-roi/.

19. American Law Institute, *Corporate Governance: Analysis and Recommendations* 2.01, Reporter's Note 29, 2.01(b)(2)-(3) and Comment d.

20. The classic work on stakeholder analysis is R. Edward Freeman, *Strategic Management: A Stakeholder Approach* (Boston: Pittman, 1984). Its ideas significantly influenced subsequent work in a wide range of fields, such as project management, conflict resolution, business-government relations, and strategic planning. Freeman's book was updated in 2013; see R. Edward Freeman, *Strategic Management: A Stakeholder Approach* (Cambridge, UK: Cambridge University Press, 2013).

21. Captain Renault to Rick, *Casablanca*, Julius & Philip Epstein, screenwriters (Hal B. Wallis Production, 1942).

22. See Virginia Postrel, *The Future and Its Enemies* (New York: Free Press, 2011).

23. Looking even more broadly, the stakeholder view may reflect a recent, now bygone era in American capitalism—a time of stability when

companies had long-term shareholders, a limited number of domestic competitors, a few government regulators, and stable employees represented by a union. These parties could be viewed benignly as important partners working together to meet the ongoing needs of their societies or as an "iron triangle" that collaborated on narrow shared interests. Both perspectives have important elements of truth, but they may also reflect an era that is now ending. An important example of the iron triangle view is Gordon Adams, *The Politics of Defense Contracting: The Iron Triangle* (New York: Council on Economic Priorities, 1981). More recently, scholars have argued for a more complex view of American business-government relationships, ranging from situations in which industries may have "captured" their government regulators to valuable, exemplary relationships that served the public interest. See David Carpenter and David Moss, *Preventing Regulatory Capture: Special Interest Influence and How to Limit It* (Cambridge, UK: Cambridge University Press, 2014).

24. Burke wrote, referring to the French revolutionaries of the late eighteenth century, "All the decent drapery of life is to be rudely torn off. All the superadded ideas, furnished from the wardrobe of a moral imagination, which the heart owns, and the understanding ratifies, as necessary to cover the defects of our naked shivering nature, and to raise it to dignity in our own estimation, are to be exploded as a ridiculous, absurd, and antiquated fashion." Edmund Burke, *Reflections on the Revolution in France* (1790; London: Seeley, Jackson, and Halliday, 1872), 75. The concept of moral imagination is multifaceted, and a conceptual and historical overview is David Bromwich, *Moral Imagination* (Princeton, NJ: Princeton University Press, 2014), 3–40.

25. Stuart Hampshire, *Innocence and Experience* (Cambridge, MA: Harvard University Press, 1991), 90.

26. A similar analysis of basic rights and duties—described as "core values" reflecting a global "overlapping consensus" and accompanied by detailed practical guidance for business managers—is Thomas Donaldson, "Values in Tension: Ethics Away from Home," *Harvard Business Review*, September–October 1996, https://hbr.org/1996/09/values-in-tension-ethics-away-from-home.

27. Smith published *The Theory of Moral Sentiments* before *The Wealth of Nations*, and he returned to it in the years before his death.

The idea that it was his prized achievement appears in Gertrude Himmelfarb, *The Roads to Modernity: The British, French, and American Enlightenments* (New York: Vintage, 2005), 35.

28. Adam Smith, *The Theory of Moral Sentiments* (Cambridge: Cambridge University Press, 2002), 229.

29. Ibid., 157.

30. E. O. Wilson, *The Social Conquest of Earth* (New York: Liveright Publishing Company, 2013), 62.

31. *Rabbi Louis Jacobs: The Preeminent Rabbi of First Century Palestine*, My Jewish Learning, http://www.myjewishlearning.com/article/hillel/ (accessed 7/10/15). Reprinted from *The Jewish Religion: A Companion* (Oxford/New York: Oxford University Press, 1995).

32. The Gospel of Matthew says, "Therefore all things whatsoever ye would that men should do to you, do ye even so to them: for this is the law and the prophets" (Matthew 7:12 [King James Version]), and the Gospel of Mark says, "And as ye would that men should do to you, do ye also to them likewise" (Luke 6:31 [King James Version]).

33. The Confucian tradition embraces a similar principal. For example, when asked if there was a single word that could serve as a rule of practice for life, Confucius is said to have replied, "Is not *shu* such a word? What you do not want done to yourself, do not do to others." See Antonio Cua, *Dimensions of Moral Creativity* (University Park: Pennsylvania State University Press, 1978), 56. Other examples are cited in Michael Shermer, *The Science of Good and Evil: Why People Cheat, Gossip, Care, Share, and Follow the Golden Rule* (New York: Times Books, 2005), 25–26. Not only has the Golden Rule been widely "discovered" and promulgated, but it plausibly serves as the foundation for a wide range of ethical theories. Philosopher Simon Blackburn, for example, suggests reasons to think that the Golden Rule forms a significant part of the underpinning of Immanuel Kant's ethical basic ethical theory. See Simon Blackburn, *Being Good* (Oxford: Oxford University Press, 2001), 116–119.

34. Bryn Zeckhauser and Aaron Sandoski, *How the Wise Decide* (New York: Random House, 2008), 160.

35. This way of using the first two questions is a version of Robert Nozick's account of rights as side constraints. See Robert Nozick, *Anarchy, State, and Utopia* (New York: Basic Books, 1974), 28–30.

Notes

Chapter Four

1. See Spencer Ante, *Creative Capital: George Doriot and the Birth of Venture Capital* (Boston: Harvard Business School Press, 2008).

2. Personal communication to author from various Harvard Business School faculty members.

3. "Planning and Procrastination: An A–Z of Business Quotations, *The Economist*, October 5, 2012, http://www.economist.com/blogs/schumpeter/2012/10/z-business-quotations.

4. Thomas Babington Macaulay, *Critical and Historical Essays* (1843; Chestnut Hill, MA: Adamant Media Corporation, 2001), 62.

5. There are many different accounts of Machiavelli's thinking. And there is also the problem of taking Machiavelli's comments and ideas, which he developed for political leaders, and applying them more broadly. The basic reason is that, as Max Weber emphasized, political leaders often make decisions involving the use of violence. In Weber's view, "It is the specific means of legitimate violence as such in the hand of human associations which determines the peculiarity of all ethical problems of politics." See Max Weber, *From Max Weber: Essays in Sociology* (London: Routledge, 2009), 124. The approach here draws heavily on Isaiah Berlin, "The Originality of Machiavelli," in *Against the Current: Essays in the History of Ideas*, ed. Henry Hardy (Princeton, NJ: Princeton University Press, 2013), 33–100.

6. Ibid., 63.

7. Mark Twain, *The Wit and Wisdom of Mark Twain: A Book of Quotations*, ed. Alex Ayres (Mineola, NY: Dover Publications, 1998), 12.

8. Cicero, *De Officiis*, quoted in Sir William Gurney Benham, *A Book of Quotations, Proverbs, and Household Words* (Philadelphia: JP Lippincott, 1907), 60.

9. This is variously attributed to Benjamin Franklin, Edgar Allan Poe, and sometimes to unnamed Italian aphorists. According to *The Oxford Dictionary of Phrase and Fable*, "Believe nothing of what you hear, and only half of what you see" dates from the mid-nineteenth century; a related Middle English saying warns that you should not believe everything that is said or that you hear, and a letter of the late eighteenth century says, "You must not take everything to be true that is told to

you." See Elizabeth Knowles, *The Oxford Dictionary of Phrase and Fable*, Encyclopedia.com., 2006, http://www.encyclopedia.com/doc/1O21 4-blvnthngfwhtyhrndnlyhlffw.html.

10. Alfred Lord Tennyson, "In Memoriam A. H. H.," 1850, http://www.portablepoetry.com/poems/alfredlord_tennyson/in_memoriam_ahh____. html. Canto 56 refers to man,

> *Who trusted God was love indeed*
> *And love Creation's final law*
> *Tho' Nature, red in tooth and claw*
> *With ravine, shriek'd against his creed.*

11. Even some of our "exemplary" behavior confirms this view. From the perspective of evolution and survival, our conscience isn't our reliable internal indicator of what is right and wrong. It is also an instrument for pursuing self-interest. As one scholar put it, the evolutionary conscience is "the still, small voice that tells us how far we can go in serving our own interests without incurring intolerable risks" (see Kyle Summers and Bernard Krespi, *Human Social Evolution: The Foundation Works of Richard D. Alexander* [Oxford: Oxford University Press, 2013], 226). For some evolutionists, religion itself is basically a solution to the problem of dealing with aggressive, alpha males in the worst-case situations when no one was around to monitor them and punish misbehavior. In this view, the gods of ancient religions, and perhaps of modern ones as well, function as "unseen enforcers"—they observe and punish antisocial behavior that society cannot observe and sanction until it's too late (see Philip Kitcher, *The Ethical Project* [Cambridge, MA: Harvard University Press, 2011], 230).

12. Leslie Stevenson and David Haberman, *Ten Theories of Human Nature* (Oxford: Oxford University Press, 2008), 54.

13. There were, of course, other ancient Chinese philosophers with different views, but nevertheless a strong theme in their thinking was that, given human nature, the state had to play a strong role to assure civilized behavior. According to Xunzi, for example, wise rulers succeeded only because they knew that, without state power, humans would be violent, disorderly, and perverse. See Herbert Plutschow, "Xunzi and the Ancient Chinese Philosophical Debate on Human Nature," *Anthropoetics* 8, no. 1 (Spring–Summer 2002), http://www.anthropoetics.ucla.edu/ap0801/xunzi.htm.

14. Philip Martin McCaulay, *Sun Tzu's the Art of War* (Raleigh, NC: Lulu Press, 2009), 25.

15. Giambattista Vico, *New Science: Principles of the New Science Concerning the Common Nature of Nations*, trans. David Marsh (1725; New York: Penguin, 2001), 78.

16. Stuart Hampshire, *Innocence and Experience* (Cambridge, MA: Harvard University Press, 1991), 170.

17. Niccolò Machiavelli, *Mandragola* (The Mandrake), trans. Stark Young (1524; New York: Macaulay, 1927), 22.

18. This is a version of what is standard analysis in international relations. Sometimes called *realpolitik*, it originated with Thucydides, was elaborated by Machiavelli, and later systematized by Hans Morgenthau and others. Recently, Harvard professor Joseph Nye coined the expression "soft power" and elaborated the distinction between it and hard power. See Joseph S. Nye Jr., *Soft Power: The Means to Success in World Politics* (New York: Public Affairs, 2009).

19. Michel de Montaigne, *The Complete Essays of Michel de Montaigne*, trans. Donald Frame (Stanford, CA: Stanford University Press, 1958), 393.

20. Hans Emil Klein, *Interactive Teaching and Emerging Technologies* (Needham, MA: World Association for Case Method Research & Application, 1996), 223.

21. Niccolò Machiavelli, *The Prince*, trans. George Bull (1532; New York: Penguin Classics, 2003), 99.

22. Robert Weisman, "Biogen Reports Death of Patient on its MS Pill," *Boston Globe*, October 22, 2014, B7.

23. Machiavelli, *The Prince*, chapter 18.

24. Ibid., 100ff.

25. See, for example, Tim Parks, *Medici Money: Banking, Metaphysics, and Art in Fifteenth-Century Florence* (New York: W. W. Norton & Company, 2005).

Chapter Five

1. William H. Whyte Jr., *The Organization Man* (Garden City, NY: Doubleday Anchor Books, 1956).

2. The statement expresses the central idea of a philosophical and religious perspective that originated in southern Africa and has recently

begun spreading through the African continent. See Michael Jesse Battle, *Reconciliation: The Ubuntu Theology of Desmond Tutu* (Cleveland: Pilgrim Press, 2009).

3. This is Godwin's version of this situation: "In a loose and general view I and my neighbour are both of us men; and of consequence entitled to equal attention. But, in reality, it is probable that one of us is a being of more worth and importance than the other. A man is of more worth than a beast; because, being possessed of higher faculties, he is capable of a more refined and genuine happiness. In the same manner the illustrious archbishop of Cambray was of more worth than his valet, and there are few of us that would hesitate to pronounce, if his palace were in flames, and the life of only one of them could be preserved, which of the two ought to be preferred." See William Godwin, *Enquiry Concerning Political Justice* (1793; Oxford: Clarendon Press, 1971), 70.

4. The philosopher John Rawls provides a basic definition of constitutive relationships, even though he did not explicitly use that terminology:

> Citizens may have, and normally do have at any given time, affections, devotions and loyalties that they believe they would not, and indeed could and should not, stand apart from and objectively evaluate from this point of view of their purely rational good. They may regard it as simply unthinkable to view themselves apart from certain religious, philosophical, and moral convictions or from certain enduring attachments and loyalties. These attachments and loyalties . . . [help] to organize and give shape to a person's life, what one sees oneself as doing and trying to accomplish in one's social world. We think that if we were suddenly without these particular convictions and attachments we would be disoriented and unable to carry on. In fact, there would be, we might think, no point in carrying on.

See John Rawls, *Collected Papers*, ed. Samuel Freeman (Cambridge, MA: Harvard University Press, 1999), 405. A counterpart to this way of thinking, in the field of game theory, is the idea that individuals define their aims partly in terms of the achievement of group goals. The concept of *team reasoning* is developed at length in Michael Bacharach, *Beyond*

Individual Choice: Teams and Choice in Game Theory, ed. Natalie Gold and Robert Sugden (Princeton, NJ: Princeton University Press, 2006).

5. Abraham Lincoln, *Lincoln's Gettysburg Oration and First and Second Inaugural Addresses* (New York: Duffield & Co., 1907), 35.

6. Philip Selznick, *TVA and the Grass Roots: A Study in the Sociology of Formal Organization* (Berkeley: University of California Press, 1949), 181.

7. Blaise Pascal, *Pensées and Other Writings*, ed. Anthony Levi, trans. Honor Levi (Oxford: Oxford University Press, 1995), 158.

8. Leslie Stevenson and David Haberman, *Ten Theories of Human Nature* (Oxford: Oxford University Press, 2008), 51, Kindle edition. A striking contemporary argument that may echo the ancient Hindu belief that "all beings and all Being are one" is Thomas Nagel, *Mind and Cosmos: Why the Materialist Neo-Darwinian Conception of Nature Is Almost Certainly False* (New York: Oxford University Press, 2012).

9. Translators have tried to convey this idea by using different terms, but their basic aim is to convey that human beings—by their nature and, more specifically, because they have the capacity for complex communication through language—tend to live in groups. This enables them to perform activities and live lives that would be impossible for them as individuals, because individual human beings are not self-sufficient. See Fred Miller, "Aristotle's Political Theory," in *The Stanford Encyclopedia of Philosophy*, ed. Edward N. Zalta (Fall 2012 edition), http://plato. stanford.edu/archives/fall2012/entries/aristotle-politics/.

10. Martin Luther King Jr., *Letter from the Birmingham Jail* (New York: Harper Collins, 1994), 4.

11. Over the following centuries, this image faded but the core idea of the unity of all humanity endured. In the Catholic tradition, for example, one of the most important social encyclicals, *Populorum Progresso*, says, "There can be no progress towards the complete development of individuals without the simultaneous development of all humanity in the spirit of solidarity. As we said at Bombay: 'Man must meet man, nation meet nation, as brothers and sisters, as children of God. In this mutual understanding and friendship, in this sacred communion, we must also begin to work together to build the common future of the human race.'" See Pope Paul VI, *Populorum Progresso*, http://www.newadvent.org/library/docs_pa06pp.htm.

12. Albert Einstein, "Religion and Science," *The New York Times Magazine*, November 9, 1930, 1.

13. Franz de Waal is a Dutch primatologist. In his book *Age of Empathy: Nature's Lessons for a Kinder Society* (New York: Harmony Books, 2009), he summarizes decades of research in the conclusion that empathy is an instinctual behavior. He then argues, like Hume and Confucius, that the ability to identify with another person's emotions may form the core of most ethical behavior. Biology doesn't prove, but it does suggest, plausible causes and influences. To the extent we have evolved as social creatures, certain ways of thinking and acting may "come naturally." This suggests that, when we think about hard decisions, we should look beyond what each of us *as individuals* should think and do.

14. Michael Newton, *Savage Boys and Wild Girls: A History of Feral Children* (London: Faber and Faber, 2002).

15. Philip Selznick, *The Moral Commonwealth* (Berkeley: University of California Press, 1992), 123.

16. Yahoo! Inc., "Yahoo Our Beliefs as a Global Internet Company," press release, February 2006, http://yahoo.client.shareholder.com/press/releasedetail.cfm?ReleaseID=187401.

17. Historians and others continue to debate how widely shared these values were. Some argue that many Germans—along with people in other countries and their governments—did not understand the Nazi threat or refused, for various reasons, to take it seriously or were intimidated into acquiescing in the Nazi agenda. See, for example, Erik Larson, *In the Garden of Beasts: Love, Terror, and an American Family in Berlin* (New York: Broadway Books, 2012). Others have argued that the Nazi takeover reflected long-standing and widely share national values. See, for example, Daniel Jonah Goldhagen, *Hitler's Willing Executioners: Ordinary Germans and the Holocaust* (New York: Vintage, 2007).

18. The translation of this statement is by Henry Hazlitt and appears in John Owen, *The Skeptics of the French Renaissance* (New York: Macmillan & Co., 1898), 466.

19. An in-depth account of our tribal instincts in evolutionary, neurological, and social terms is Joshua Greene, *Moral Tribes: Emotion, Reason, and the Gap Between Us and Them* (New York: Penguin Press, 2013).

20. This was the title of Nietzsche's book of aphorisms; the full title is *Menschliches, Allzumenschliches: Ein Buch für freie Geister* (Human, All Too Human: A Book for Free Spirits) (1878).

21. Chester I. Barnard, *The Functions of the Executive* (Cambridge, MA: Harvard University Press, 1971), 239.

22. An extended analysis of Holmes's way of thinking, which draws on contemporary psychology and neuroscience, is Maria Konnikova, *Mastermind: How to Think Like Sherlock Holmes* (New York: Penguin, 2013).

23. An excellent introduction to design thinking is Tim Brown, *Change by Design* (New York: Harper Collins Publishers, 2009).

24. Personal observation by author.

25. Abraham Edel, *Aristotle and His Philosophy* (Piscataway, NJ: Transaction Publishers, 1995), 9–11.

26. A wide-ranging literature review of the narrative perspective and the "social construction" of reality is Jerome Bruner, "The Narrative Construction of Reality," *Critical Inquiry* 18, no. 1 (Autumn 1991): 1–21.

27. Adrienne Rich, "Love Poem II," in *Selected Poems* (New York: W. W. Norton & Co., 2013), 54.

28. Oliver Wendell Holmes Jr., *The Common Law* (1881; Mineola NY: Dover Publications, 1991), 1.

29. See *The Holmes-Pollock Letters: The Correspondence of Mr. Justice Holmes and Sir Frederick Pollock, 1874 1932*, 2nd ed., ed. Mark De Wolfe Howe (Cambridge, MA, Belknap Press of Harvard University Press, 1961), 109.

Chapter Six

1. A recent, comprehensive review of the philosophical and management literature on management judgment is John Shotter and Haridimos Tsoukas, "In Search of Phronesis: Leadership and the Art of Judgment," *Academy of Management Learning & Education* 13, no. 2 (June 2014): 224–243.

2. Gautama Buddha, "Sermon at Benares," in *Speeches in World History*, ed. Suzanne McIntire (New York: Facts on File, 2009), 13.

3. Confucius, *Confucius: Confucian Analects, The Great Learning and the Doctrine of the Mean*, trans. James Legge (New York: Dover Publications, 1971), 395. An extensive treatment of the inevitability

of judgment about particular situations in the Confucian tradition is
Antonio Cua, *Dimensions of Moral Creativity* (University Park, PA:
Pennsylvania State University Press, 1978).

4. Moses Maimonides, "Mishneh Torah: Laws of Ethical Conduct,"
in Hal M. Lewis, *From Sanctuary to Boardroom: A Jewish Approach to
Leadership* (Lanham, MD: Rowman & Littlefield Publishers, 2006), 134.

5. A religious principle of balance appears often in contemporary
explanations of Islam and studies in comparative religion. The quotation above is a translation of a saying attributed to Mohammad: "خير
الأمور الوسط," *Wikipedia*, http://en.wikipedia.org/wiki/Golden_mean_
(philosophy), retrieved 09/25/2014.

6. Alexander Nehamas, *Nietzsche: Life as Literature* (Cambridge,
MA: Harvard University Press, 1987), 158.

7. Sloan's impact on twentieth-century management is described in
detail in Alfred Chandler, *Strategy and Structure: Chapters in the History of
American Industrial Enterprise* (Washington DC: The Beard Group, 1962).

8. Alfred P. Sloan, *My Years with General Motors* (New York: Crown
Business, 1990), xxii.

9. Hemingway was writing about bullfighting, and his full statement was, "So far, about morals, I only know that what is moral is what
you feel good after and what is immoral is what you feel bad after and
judged by these moral standards, which I do not defend, the bullfight is
very moral to me because I feel very fine while it is going on and have a
feeling of life and death and mortality and immortality, and after it is
over I feel very sad but very fine." See Ernest Hemingway, *Death in the
Afternoon* (1932; New York: Scribner, 1960), 13.

10. This statement of Sartre's is a paraphrase of comment Dmitri
Karamazov makes to his brother Alyosha in *The Brothers Karamazov,* by
Fyodor Dostoyevsky. See Jean Paul Sartre, *Existentialism Is a Humanism*
(1946; New Haven: Yale University Press, 2007), 28. Sartre's statement
has been interpreted in a variety of ways, some of which are more benign
and suggest simply that human beings are free, or, as Sartre often put
it, "condemned to be free," and hence must make important choices
for themselves and not delegate them to institutions or orthodoxies. In
Being and Nothingness, Sartre writes that "my freedom is the unique
foundation of values and that *nothing*, absolutely nothing, justifies me in

adopting this or that particular value, this or that particular schedule of values." See Jean Paul Sartre, *Being and Nothingness*, trans. Hazel Barnes (1943; New York: Washington Square Press, 1966), 76.

11. Barbara McKinnon, ed., *American Philosophy: A Historical Anthology* (Albany, NY: State University of New York Press, 1985), 46.

12. William Shakespeare, *Measure for Measure* (*The Riverside Shakespeare*, ed. G. Blakemore Evans [Boston: Houghton Mifflin Company, 1974]), act 2, scene 2, lines 114–123.

13. Ignatius of Loyola, *The Spiritual Exercises and Selected Works*, ed. George E. Ganss, S.J. (Mahwah, NJ: Paulist Press, 1991).

14. William Shakespeare, *Macbeth* (*The Riverside Shakespeare*, ed. G. Blakemore Evans [Boston: Houghton Mifflin Company, 1974]), act 2, scene 3, line 111.

15. Michael Walzer, *Just and Unjust Wars: A Moral Argument with Historical Illustrations* (New York: Basic Books, 2010), 6.

16. William James, *Pragmatism* (1907; Buffalo, NY: Prometheus Books, 1991), 10.

17. Joseph Addison, *Cato: A Tragedy in Five Acts* (1713; Seattle: Amazon Digital Services), 18.

18. This proposition is a major theme in Daniel Gilbert, *Stumbling on Happiness* (New York: Vintage, 2006).

19. Rebecca Leung, "The Mensch of Malden Mills," *60 Minutes*, July 3, 2003, http://www.cbsnews.com/news/the-mensch-of-malden-mills/.

20. David McCullough, interview with Bruce Cole, *Humanities*, July–August 2002.

21. Guy de Maupassant, *Alien Hearts*, trans. Richard Howard (New York: New York Review of Books, 2009), 104.

22. Jim Mullen, personal communication to Professor Joshua Margolis, Harvard Business School, 2007.

23. Richard Burton, *To the Gold Coast for Gold* (London: Chatto and Windus, 1883), 59. This statement is quoted in and summarizes a basic theme of Kwame Anthony Appiah, *Cosmopolitanism: Ethics in a World of Strangers* (New York: W. W. Norton & Company, 2007).

24. David Lilienthal, *Management: A Humanist Art* (New York: Columbia University Press, 1967), 18.

25. Ibid.

Appendix A

1. Tony Davies, *Humanism* (London, England: Routledge, 1997).

Appendix B

1. Some translators convey this idea by using the word "social" instead of "political." In either case, the aim is to convey that human beings—by their nature and, more specifically, because they have the capacity for complex communication through language—naturally tend to live in groups. This enables them to perform activities and live lives that would be impossible for them as individuals, because individual human beings are not self-sufficient. See Fred Miller, "Aristotle's Political Theory," in *The Stanford Encyclopedia of Philosophy*, ed. Edward N. Zalta, Fall 2012 edition, http://plato.stanford.edu/archives/fall2012/entries/aristotle-politics/>.

2. See Alisdair MacIntyre, *Dependent Rational Animals: Why Human Beings Need the Virtues* (Chicago: Open Court Press, 1999), 55.

INDEX

Index

Index

Index

ACKNOWLEDGMENTS

For more than a decade, I have had the great good fortune, personally and professionally, of working with a remarkable group of colleagues on an important challenge. Together, we have designed and taught a course called Leadership and Corporate Accountability. This is a required course for all nine hundred students in the first year of the Harvard MBA program, and it teaches them about the economic, legal, and ethical responsibilities they will take on as managers.

For me, working with the LCA group has been a decade-long seminar in the conceptual, historical, legal, and practical aspects of making hard, important decisions in organizations. Some of my colleagues in this group came from a range of traditional academic disciplines, and others had years of experience as managers and executives. As a result, when I began writing about gray area problems, I drew heavily on all I had learned from these colleagues, and that is why this book is dedicated to them.

In addition, a number of my colleagues have read drafts of this book, and their suggestions improved it significantly. I am particularly indebted to Lena Goldberg, Richard Hamermesh, Nien-he Hsieh, Karthik Ramanna, Joshua

Margolis, Henry McGee, Lynn Paine, Sandra Sucher, Clayton Rose, and Ken Winston.

From the beginning to the end of this project, my editor, Melinda Merino, made innumerable valuable suggestions, as did Rafe Sagalyn and Jerry Useem at critical junctures.

My family was also involved in this project from start to finish. My daughters, Maria, Luisa, and Gabriella, and my sons-in-law, Lee Lockwood and Michael Duffy, all provided encouragement and ideas. Finally, over several years, my wife, Patricia O'Brien, patiently listened to my ideas about this book and read several drafts of it. She provided encouragement, criticism, suggestions, corrections, and many valuable ideas that contributed immeasurably to this effort.

ABOUT THE AUTHOR

Joseph L. Badaracco is the John Shad Professor of Business Ethics at Harvard Business School, where he teaches in the school's MBA and executive programs. In recent years, Professor Badaracco served as head of the MBA program and head of the Harvard University Advisory Committee on Shareholder Responsibility. He has taught in executive programs in the United States, Japan, and other countries. Badaracco is the author of several books on leadership, decision making, and responsibility. These include *Defining Moments: When Managers Must Choose between Right and Right*; *Leading Quietly: An Unorthodox Guide to Doing the Right Thing*; *Questions of Character: Illuminating the Heart of Leadership through Literature*; and *The Good Struggle: Responsible Leadership in an Unforgiving World*. These books have been translated into ten languages. Badaracco is a graduate of St. Louis University, Oxford University, where he was a Rhodes scholar, and Harvard Business School, where he earned an MBA and a DBA.